GW00731953

WITHDRAWN

THE QUEST OF SIMON RICHARDSON

THE QUEST OF
SIMON RICHARDSON

A BIOGRAPHY

by

DOROTHY RICHARDSON

together with
A VOYAGE IN *Baroque* WITH H. W. TILMAN IN 1973
by Simon Richardson

Foreword by Anthony Quinton

LONDON
VICTOR GOLLANCZ LTD
1986

First published in Great Britain 1986
by Victor Gollancz Ltd,
14 Henrietta Street, London WC2E 8QJ

© Dorothy Richardson 1986

British Library Cataloguing in Publication Data
Richardson, Dorothy
  The quest of Simon Richardson: a biography.
  1. Richardson, Simon   2. Seamen—
  England—Biography
  I. Title   II. Richardson, Simon
  910.4'5'0924   G464

  ISBN 0-575-03853-5

Typeset at The Spartan Press Limited, Lymington, Hants,
and printed in Great Britain by
St Edmundsbury Press, Bury St Edmunds, Suffolk
Illustrations originated and printed by Thomas Campone, Southampton

This book is dedicated
to everyone who loved Simon
and the men who sailed with him
in *En Avant* for the Antarctic.

Once the realization is accepted that even between the closest human beings infinite distances continue to exist, a wonderful living side by side can grow up, if they succeed in loving the distance between them which makes it possible for each to see the other whole against the sky.

RAINER MARIA RILKE

CONTENTS

LIST OF ILLUSTRATIONS

following page 110

Claude Richardson (*photo Hubert Galsworthy*)

Dorothy Richardson with Selina and Simon (1954) (*photo Hubert Galsworthy*)

Simon aged 2 (*photo Hubert Galsworthy*)

Simon aged 4 (*photo Hubert Galsworthy*)

Simon aged 8

Simon aged 13

Simon aged 20, on board *Baroque* (*photo Ilan Rosengarten*)

On Mount Change, Greenland (*photo David Meldrum*)

Simon aged 22, with Mark Johnson (*photo Christopher Lloyd Owen*)

2 days before the accident: Paddy Tritton and Simon preparing to go fishing on the Spey (*photo Veronica Tritton*)

Simon in bed after the accident negotiating on the telephone for *En Avant* (*photo Robin Evelyn*)

Simon convalescing (*photo Veronica Tritton*)

En Avant as she was when bought (*photo collection Nationaal Sleepvaart Museum, Maasluis/Holland*)

En Avant, with her superstructure removed, arriving in Southampton Water (*photo Robin Evelyn*)

En Avant in Smith's boatyard, Southampton (*photo Robin Evelyn*)

En Avant the day she left for Rio (*photo Southern Newspapers plc*)

Mark Johnson, H. W. Tilman, and Simon at the tiller, as *En Avant* moves off; in the bow: Joe Dittamore and Rod Coatman (*photo Southern Newspapers plc*)

Joe Dittamore, Robert Toombs, Charles Williams and Rod Coatman leaving Southampton (*photo Southern Newspapers plc*)

ACKNOWLEDGEMENTS

The loving support of the families of Simon's companions has been a continuing comfort to me, and I shall always be grateful. Also to Nicolas and Frances McDowall, without whose help and encouragement this book would never have been written. The first draft was a straightforward biography, written impersonally; when I showed it to them they told me I had written the wrong book, and advised me (it seemed as if they gave me permission) to rewrite it from my own point of view. This I have found very rewarding, and I am grateful to them.

Many other people have played a considerable part in it, and I hope I have adequately expressed my thanks to them: Janine Barbereau, Alan Cowley, Geoffrey Hattersley-Smith, John Heap, Jean and Michael Johnson, John Mead, Libby Purves, Tony Quinton, Hilary Rubinstein and Jo Stevens. I would also like to thank those who have allowed me to use their material: Angus Clarke, Pam Davis, Kenneth Hesketh, David Lewis, Christopher Lloyd Owen, David Meldrum, Colin Putt, Freda Rawlings, Michael Richey, Henry Thompson and Veronica Tritton.

Above all, I want to acknowledge the part played by the shadowy figure of Claude Richardson. Everyone who knew and loved him will recognise how much Simon owed to his father, and that this book is a celebration of both their lives.

D.R.

FOREWORD

SIMON RICHARDSON WAS a modest, private person, with a kind of reticence that used to be thought characteristically British. In the narrative that follows of his trip to Greenland with H. W. Tilman in 1973, he instantly qualifies any tendency to unfavourable judgement of Joyce's *Ulysses* by admitting the likelihood of his own misunderstanding. This, we should remember, applies to one of the last books one would have expected to be carried for recreational purposes on a small boat in winds which seem all too often to be Force 7. A lesser man might have chucked it over the side in the circumstances.

Of Tilman himself his criticisms are always contained within a framework of admiration. Only one of the crew comes in for anything like punitive judgement: his combined faults being the avoidance of work and complaining. In fastening on these weaknesses Simon Richardson goes against the common idea that the shortcomings we notice most readily in others are our own. He was a prodigious worker and, as is shown by the way he triumphed over his dreadful accident in 1975, in the matter of refusal to complain he leaves the legendary Spartan boy with the fox under his coat lumbering feebly in the rear. His contempt for dark glasses is very much of a piece with that.

Simon's intense distaste for making any sort of show of himself is altogether congruous with his having been at school at Winchester. Not all Wykehamists, furthermore, slide into permanent under-secretaryships of state in their forgettable dark suits. Mallory, who was last seen 'going strong', 800 feet below the summit of Everest in June, 1924, came to the school as a scholar in 1900.

The smashing of his leg in Scotland would seem to have driven out of Simon's head the thought of any career but a life of action in the open, a resourceful combat with nature. Even before that, the style of his intentions is clear from the Greenland narrative. Not only is Tilman's boat, *Baroque*, in a pretty ruinous condition and in need of continuous improvisation and sensitive attention, which Simon carried out with obviously craftsmanly competence in fairly repellent conditions of sea and temperature; arriving at Upernivik, about the furthest point north in their expedition, he goes off for a day with a friend made there, to climb a mountain never before climbed from sea level and returns very late after nineteen hours of continuous exercise, which elicits from him the comment 'quite a feat, I thought.'

In the Greenland narrative the idea of becoming a writer comes briefly to the surface from time to time. He writes of the narrative itself as his 'novel' and makes calculations about what would be needed in the way of wordage and rate of output. A writerly seriousness reveals itself in various forms. The more literary element in the ship's rather interesting freight of reading matter is treated with care and respect, even in the cases where he does not much like it. In explaining his dissatisfaction with Saint-Exupéry he preaches his own admirably concrete practice in objecting to the Frenchman's tendency to gaseous abstraction. The detective stories on board are left to the end and a Nicolas Freeling is dismissed as 'very bad'.

His own practice in its plainness and objectivity is, of course, as with George Orwell, a strategem of self-effacement. Both seem to have thought of themselves as perfectly ordinary. It is enough to consider the world as they report it to see that they were not. Simon is often funny, sometimes a little rueful, extraordinarily unpetty and unquerulous. The writing is hardly ever colourful or showy. On the few occasions where it is, it is so in an attractively self-mocking fashion, and the character that emerges from what he writes, and from the detailed account of the aftermath of his accident and of the purchase and preparation of *En Avant* for his last voyage, comes as no surprise. Some of his superb calmness and resolution may have been connected with the fact that he was a quite exceptionally good-looking man. The eighteen-year-old girl who pressed herself upon him in Umanak may have smelt of drink but she knew what she was about.

But, of course, there was much more to him than that. He was, innately, someone who *did* things. In the agonizing course of his coping with the injury to his leg, it is almost a relief to read that, when he came round at one point, he asked if there was a telephone for the patients. He was told that it was broken, so he dismantled it, reassembled the pieces and rang his home.

As a contrast to the people who first broke the telephone and their associates who failed to see that it was repaired or failed to repair it, it is pleasant to read that his superbly worded advertisement in one Saturday's *Times* — Crew wanted for Antarctic voyage — elicited 160 replies.

It is entirely natural to regret the loss of such a remarkable person at such a very early age. But in a way it is not sensible. Simon Richardson was made the very special man he was by his courage, his determination, his readiness to take risks. They were, as he knew very well, real risks and what makes risks real is the chance they carry with them of disaster. The accident to his leg in 1975 was simply an accident, not reasonably to be expected, simply a random happening. The extraordinary energies it released in him enabled him consciously to take the chance of the voyage he planned to Smith Island in the Antarctic.

The last word from him in the letter to his mother from Las Palmas is in every way characteristic: the practical requests for sail needles, primus stove and beeswax; the word of thanks to be given to the sailmaker for the excellence of his sails; the calm, the resolve. I am grateful for what, with courteous indirectness, he lets us get to know about himself in the pages that follow.

TRINITY COLLEGE, OXFORD   ANTHONY QUINTON
JULY 1983

THE QUEST OF SIMON RICHARDSON

IT MUST HAVE been during the winter of 1981/82 that I discovered Simon's Journal in his little writing-case. By then he would probably have been dead several years, long enough for us to have been able to get a legal presumption of death. I remember that I was alone in the house and it was quite late at night. It was after we had built on the other staircase and the garden room and divided the house into two, and Selina and John and the boys had moved in; but at the time that I found the Journal John was at sea and Selina and the boys were away, so I was alone in the whole house except for the dogs.

Simon's writing-case, a birthday present of his schooldays, was the last of his belongings that I had to deal with. Most of his clothes I had put into plastic sacks for the dustman: shrunken remains of his youth, boiler suits stiff with diesel and engine grease, odd halves of pyjamas, several left shoes and boots which were relicts of his accident, shabby Old Wykehamist ties. The dinner-jacket and the wedding garment handed down from some old great-uncle, which he enjoyed peacocking in once in a while, were still hanging in his cupboard waiting like Cinderella's slipper for someone whom they fitted to turn up, and the collection of fishing flies and little bits of engines were collecting dust in the Mill. Only the writing-case remained, the last invasion of his privacy. When Dicky died Simon went to his desk and sorted through it, no doubt feeling that fathers sometimes left skeletons like jacks-in-the-box, and it was a son's duty to field them. Now there was no one here to do this but me.

Dicky is Claude Richardson who died in 1974, Selina is our first child born in 1947 and now married to John Musters, Commander R.N., with James and Charles born in '75 and '78. Home is Longstock Mill, in Hampshire, which has been home for almost all my married life. Our other child, Simon, was born in 1952 and this book is really about him, a voyage of discovery about him, which started that evening when I opened his case. Inside it was a manuscript, 50 foolscap pages in Simon's tiniest writing, curling at the edges and spattered with sea water. Undated, no heading or title, it started 'The Old Man is definitely unhappy at the moment' and I realized that it must be about the voyage he made to the Arctic in 1973 with H. W. Tilman, the Old Man, in Tilman's boat *Baroque*. Page after page of intense writing, grubby and smudged, with now and then a diagram or a page of calculations.

This may not sound very dramatic. Many unexpected manuscripts have been found after their authors' deaths; but I had never known Simon willingly to put pen to paper — in fact, we were given to understand that at Winchester he was considered to be illiterate — and to discover that he could keep up what seemed to be a journal, day after day, in neat small writing, was a revelation and a most exciting one. When later I deciphered the manuscript and put it into readable form the character of the author that emerged was so unlike the public face which he showed the world that I began to feel that my spectacles hadn't been so rose-tinted after all; indeed, I may have underestimated the capability and the perception. I wondered how much more there was to understand of my son, and how I could set about finding it out. Anything connected with Simon has always been tremendously exciting to me: his vitality was like a glass of champagne and he made life very easy and pleasant. On the day that his expedition sailed I could have burst with pride, and that feeling has remained with me through all the uncertainties since. When I found the manuscript I simply saw it as an opening for knowing more about him, but as events developed I found myself caught up, not by my own volition, into chronicling the story of his life; I was not pushing, just responding to events, so that it seemed to be what Quakers would call 'in right ordering' to do so.

I thought it would be a good discipline to transfer Simon's journal to typescript as I read it, rather than try to read it straight through. I hoped the interest of the narrative would carry me on, so I set up my typewriter at the end of the dining table and worked at it whenever I had any spare time. The writing was so small, and the greek 'e's and odd 'r's so difficult to read that it was slow work, but I enjoyed it, because Simon wrote exactly as he spoke, and working on it made him feel very close. I hadn't done very much, perhaps ten pages, when on 18 January I had an unexpected letter that opened the next door. It was from a television producer in Cardiff:

Dear Dorothy Richardson,

Last year I made a documentary for ITV entitled 'It's a Bit British' of the Three Peaks Yacht Race. This race was inspired by Major H. W. Tilman, whom I believe you knew.

I am now actively investigating the possibility of a documentary about Bill Tilman himself. Through the kind offices of Mrs P. Davis, I have obtained a fair amount of photographic and written material about his exploits over a period of forty years. I now wish to cast the net a little wider to see if we can obtain further photographic, written or audio material, and, in particular, talk to some of the people who knew him well during his lifetime.

I wonder if it would be possible for you to help in any of these ways? I am particularly interested in talking to members of his crew during his various voyages on *Mischief, Sea Breeze* and *Baroque*.

I would be delighted to hear from you if you feel you can help me in any way. Please do not hesitate to write or telephone reversing the charge.

Yours sincerely,

John Mead

Producer/Director

I replied inviting him to lunch, and it was arranged that he should come early in March. When the day came I enjoyed our meeting very much indeed. John Mead has the gift, essential I imagine in a television interviewer, of easy communication; and once he realized that I was not going to get emotional at the mention of Simon's name — rather the reverse, I was happy to talk about him and his expedition — a quick intimacy was established. A sailor himself, he could appreciate the development of relationships in a small boat, and was clearly intrigued to understand why such a famous skipper as Tilman should sail as crew with someone of twenty-four. This of course has interested many people, and must have contributed considerably to the publicity about Simon's disappearance.

It seemed that John Mead was not having much success in finding members of Tilman's crews willing or able to talk about him. Either they no longer lived in England — Colin Putt whom I had met was then in Australia, as also was Ilan Rosengarten — and it seems from some of Tilman's books that a few were less than enchanted by their experiences. When I mentioned Simon's journal John jumped at the chance of reading what had so far been typed and took a copy away. I told him about the three boxes of slides that had been sent back from Rio and offered to lend them if he wanted to use any for the film. It was altogether a very pleasant meeting and I should have been sorry not to see him again; though to him it was just part of a job, a painstaking piecing together of a fascinating life story. I was to some extent the last observer of that life, as Major Tilman spent his last few weeks in England, here, in this house.

The work of transcribing the manuscript went on, and if it hadn't been so interesting I should have found it laborious. Simon seemed to be writing it for himself, there was no hint of selfconsciousness: or perhaps it was a true reflection of an absolutely unselfconscious personality. I was still in the process of moving from the whole house, which we had bought in 1947 and made our family home, into about a third of it. This was very satisfying, because I was able to choose just the bits of furniture and pictures that I was really fond of and shed the responsibility of too much house and garden. John and Selina were settling into the rest of the house, though John, who was serving in H.M.S. *Invincible*, was away in Norway. Sometimes when Selina had a little time to spare she would come and help me by deciphering Simon's writing and dictating to me, and then I rattled along. This was March 1982, and she and the boys were looking forward to John's homecoming, and leave on a farm in Devon — which is where they were at six o'clock one morning when John was recalled to his ship to sail for the Falklands.

The Falklands war isn't part of the story at all, but it affected us profoundly, as it did every family who had a member serving there. The shock to Selina and all the other young women, the naval wives she knew, when they realized that there might be a war, that husbands and lovers were sailing thousands of miles south into danger, produced all the symptoms of depression and fear. Selina recovered marvellously, and set about organizing groups of families to meet weekly to support each other, and this was a great help both to her and to them. We listened to all the news bulletins together, and it added to the strain to hear of all the places we had learnt of in the search for *En Avant*: South Georgia, Port Stanley, Punta Arenas, Tierra del Fuego. I went on doggedly typing. It was difficult to suppress the ridiculous hope that with all the activity in those waters some news or clue might turn up, though I knew with my intelligence that there was no possibility that Simon and his crew would be found, beards down to their knees, cheerfully returning to the world.

John Mead came a second time, very welcome, talked a lot more, borrowed the slides, and asked if I would go to Cardiff to do an interview for his film. I was rather pleased to be asked; though I have always hated being photographed, I never mind talking, and talking about Simon and his expedition is a positive pleasure. It was arranged that I should go to Cardiff some time in August, when John would be interviewing various other people for the programme, including

Major Tilman's niece Pam Davis, whom I knew. John had read the first instalment of Simon's journal and seemed impressed and wanted to read more.

The jaunt to Cardiff, when it happened, was great fun because Pam and I stayed at the same hotel the night before we were needed. It was much nicer than being alone, and as Pam had made a name for herself as the women's gliding champion I felt she would know the form when it came to television interviews. We were collected after breakfast and driven to the studio, where in turn we were made up and then put to wait in an upper room. I was sent for first, and followed John's assistant Jane down a labyrinth of narrow corridors into a large dark room and into an illuminated chair, just like on Mastermind. I was pleased not to feel frightened at all, rather exhilarated, in fact. As soon as John started talking I completely forgot the surroundings — I knew there were other people there because John spoke to them, but I couldn't see anyone. John asked me questions and the conversation flowed easily, then he led up to the thousand dollar questions which he hadn't touched on before: what did I think had happened to the Expedition? What did I feel about them going? How did I feel about their loss? It was done so easily and spontaneously that I could answer quite naturally. Then there was silence. John thanked me and said that was all. Lights came on and I became aware that we were in a very large studio and there were a lot of people in the room, many more than I had imagined. Jane came up to me and hugged me and seemed much moved. I was taken back upstairs and found that Pam had been watching my interview on a television set, and then I could watch hers.

Before I left Cardiff John told me that he had been approached by Libby Purves, the writer and broadcaster, and sailor, who was collecting material for an article about Tilman and had already edited a selection of his writings. He had told her about Simon's journal, and the insights it gave into Tilman's character and the experience of sailing with him. When shortly afterwards a letter arrived from her, asking if she could come down and talk to me about it, I felt I was being carried along towards something I couldn't yet understand but didn't want to avoid, and I wrote inviting her to lunch. She came a week or two before her first child was expected, and after lunch I left her with her feet up on the sofa and the now nearly-completed typescript of Simon's journal. Her opinion of it was important to me: if a second, completely unbiased, knowledgeable person thought it was good then maybe someone, somewhere, sometime might publish it. Perhaps the story of *En Avant* could be added to the journal to tell of Simon's achievements.

Libby said she liked it, and said she certainly thought it was good. She wanted to use one or two passages in her article for the *Guardian*, and I gave permission on condition that she mentioned the finding of the journal of the voyage in *Baroque*. I drove her back to Winchester with all sorts of incredible thoughts whizzing round in my head. The article, when it appeared in the *Guardian* on Saturday, 8 January 1983, was almost an introduction to this book, and I have asked her permission to print it in full. It is a fascinating portrait of Major Tilman, and is headed 'Spartan Explorer'.

'Five years ago this winter, a remarkable chapter of maritime history came quietly to an end. The expedition ship *En Avant* — a steel tug converted to sail — set out from the Brazilian coast. She planned to call at Port Stanley for two more climbers, and to move on to attempt Smith Island in the South Shetlands — one of the most difficult and inaccessible of Antarctic peaks.

'*En Avant* sailed south from Rio de Janeiro on 1 November, 1977. Neither boat nor crew have been heard of since. The skipper, Simon Richardson, and most of his crew were young men. But lost with them, in a typically game attempt to spend his eightieth birthday in the Antarctic Circle was an old one. He was Major H. W. Tilman — to me, and to many others, one of the least recognized and most fascinating explorers of the century.

'It was ironic that after covering 140,000 miles in Arctic and Antarctic travels, and surviving two shipwrecks with boats of his own, Tilman should have vanished on an expedition of which he was not the leader. But the fact that he was invited at all, at seventy-nine, to stand his watches in such a young crew is remarkable. It throws some new light on his difficult, dry, compelling, and unique character.

'Tilman was one of the last Victorian gentleman-explorers. He shunned sponsorship, publicity, and interview. He crept back into Lymington at the end of each hair-raising voyage with the minimum of fuss. Asked once by a keen cadet, "Sir, how do I get on an expedition?" He replied curtly, "Put on your boots and go."

'He had scarcely been out of his own boots in six decades: he was a notable mountaineer in the Thirties and Forties, a soldier in both world wars, and only at the end a seafarer. Tilman took to sailing in his mid-fifties, when the high Himalayan climbs got beyond him. He replaced the challenge of immensely high mountains with the challenge of immensely remote ones. Hence his crossing of the Patagonian ice-cap from Pacific to Atlantic inlets: hence his raids on the heights and wildernesses of Arctic Greenland and Baffin Bay. Finally, the sea itself came to fascinate him: in his late seventies he was still circumnavigating Spitzbergen and making valiant attempts to thread through the pack-ice to Ellesmere Island in Baffin Bay.

'The boats he chose for his voyages were within his modest means and spartan expectations — a series of three Bristol Channel pilot cutters, none built later than 1906, and all owning idiosyncrasies and weaknesses which would give pause to many Solent yachtsmen, let alone Arctic explorers. He nursed his most famous boat, *Mischief*, through more than 100,000 sea-miles, and she bestowed her name on a mountain in each hemisphere and a cape in the Southern Ocean. *Baroque* is still afloat today; *Sea Breeze* was wrecked in 1972 in an incident which merely prompted the reflection from her owner that "for me the lesson of this sad story is not to mess about in Greenland fjords without an engine, especially when they are full of ice."

'To crew his veteran boats he placed uninviting entries in *The Times*: "Hands wanted for long voyage in small boat, no pay, no prospects, not much pleasure", or "Cook for a cold voyage: five mouths to feed for two months." His eager young crew found home-comforts scarce and the ship's management firm. Tales abound (many told by Tilman against himself) of disputes over the eating of cold curry for breakfast, of the low status of anyone soft enough to wear gloves at night, or refuse to eat sardine spines, and of the skipper's resolute refusal to stop and put ashore disaffected crews, preferring to press on for Reykjavik in the belief that they would have got used to the life by then, and stay.

'Nor did all endorse Tilman's robust and old-fashioned belief that "every herring should hang by its own tail." He did not approve of life-rafts or emergency transmitters, preferring, in remote waters, the stimulus of self-reliance. A Tilman crew was meant to leap on to an ice-floe and hack out a rudimentary mooring bollard; to tackle such backbreaking tasks as throwing out all the ballast and replacing it with stones to escape a disastrous grounding; to relish (as the skipper did) a solid and seamanlike diet of currant duff cooked in a bucket, and stews enlivened with Tabasco sauce. "No ship should be without it. It adds a relish to the plainest fare, and is probably a powerful germicide." Not surprisingly, in sailing circles, a mixed legend has grown round his name.

'I grew to know Tilman through his books. He writes in a dry, entertaining and fresh style which stands out from the turgid modern sailing literature like a beacon of scholarly sanity. When I undertook the task of selecting and editing the best from his eight voyaging books I kept away from those who had sailed with him. It seemed better to allow him to speak directly, writer to reader, than to become embroiled just then in the hundred different analyses of his character and merits. I always liked one of his favourite quotations, an Arab proverb, which he produced at every disagreement with his crews: "The camel driver has his thoughts, and the camel he has his." The works I edited were those, definitely, of the camel driver.

'However, reading his books, one cannot ignore a disturbingly Lear-like tone which develops and darkens as time goes on. Tilman was increasingly disappointed in the young companions he found so haphazardly. Apart from one disastrous voyage south, when his crew deserted him in Montevideo only to be replaced with some even more unfortunate choices (including a racing cyclist who cooked cabbage with custard, and a black Uruguayan engineer who started a knife fight on South Georgia), his complaints are fairly minor.

'He was disappointed in the new generation's apparent softness and lack of purpose in voyaging. To Bob Comlay, one of the successful crews who became a friend and long-time correspondent, he wrote crossly of a less successful mate: "He has not yet paid back any of the money I lent him . . . I am afraid he is unreliable, like too many others nowadays. I dislike being taken for a ride by a young squirt." He cheerfully encourages Comlay, trying for university, to go into the army instead and "get shot at in Ulster, where at least you would be doing some good." Later he congratulates him on graduating and finding a job . . . earning some cash. "At one time I feared you were on the way to becoming a perpetual student." The tone of alienated impatience — perhaps inevitable in one who spent his own late teenage years in the trenches, growing up too fast — is seldom far below the surface of his later writing.

'It is Simon Richardson — who crewed for him to Greenland in 1973 — who has now, years later, provided one of the most perceptive crew's-eye-views of Tilman. Richardson's mother has found, and intends eventually to publish, a journal that her son wrote during that voyage. It is one of the rare accounts of a Tilman voyage given by someone other than the skipper himself. It portrays a taciturn man, satisfied as long as the boat went well, but unwilling to indulge in man-management or any degree of tactful "jollying-along" of his very young crew. At one stage Simon, aged twenty, wrote home exasperatedly of being "miles from anywhere in a leaky boat with a grumpy old man who can't stand anybody." But gradually, a relationship developed between the old man and the boy. Simon was a born adventurer himself, active and hardy and self-assured: "When he turned on me and said, 'What the hell did you do that for, Simon?' I'd had enough. I said 'What the hell do you think I did it for?' From then on he has treated me as an equal."

'Mrs Richardson — who had Tilman to stay in the house while the fated Smith Island expedition was forming — believes that across the 60-year gap the two recognized each other. "Major Tilman saw in Simon the qualities of the born explorer. I think he was glad to find them in this generation." Simon, like Tilman, was determined to mount his own expedition, chose his own boat, financed it, did the work himself and dispensed with support-ships and much of the paraphernalia of modern exploration. He invited Tilman to join *En Avant* as a simple crew member.

'Depressed by the end of his own sailing, tempted by the Antarctic spring, the old traveller gladly threw in his lot with the young ones. When they left, Tilman was seventy-nine, his skipper only twenty-four. It was, in a way, a formidable compliment from a past age to a new one. If they had ever come home, the account of the voyage might have been a story of reconciled generations: Tilman wrote from Rio that Simon's companions were "a better lot than any I have ever had. . . ." As it is, the end of Simon's old Greenland journal is perhaps not the worst epitaph for H. W. Tilman: "He's definitely a shy man, and aggressive as many shy people get. . . . People find him intolerant, I don't think he is. He sums you up, makes an opinion and then keeps you up to it. He knows people's limitations, can and does accept them, then keeps you up to those limitations. . . . Everybody thinks of him as an ogre, and crawls around. He would much prefer it if people stood up for themselves — really stood up. He always puts in the last word — which we should not let him do."'

8 JANUARY 1983   LIBBY PURVES

Within a fortnight of the article appearing in the *Guardian* I had letters from two publishers expressing interest in the journal and asking if they might be able to see it. This made me light-headed, it all began to look too easy. the journal seemed hardly long enough to make a book, and I wanted to write the story of Simon's own achievement — or, rather, I wanted it to be written and I didn't see how anyone else could do it, because no one else knew the whole story. I decided to write a biography round the journal.

So far all I had to go on in assessing its value was the opinion of two people whom I did not really know well who had only read part of it, and who had never met Simon. I decided to ask someone whom I knew well and whose judgement I could rely on to tell me if it was worth publishing. My immediate thought was of Tony Quinton. He is a good friend of the family and quite remarkable in that his worldly success hasn't made him pompous. When Dicky died, having said twice that there was to be no religious service but that instead I was to invite all his friends to a really good concert and supper afterwards, I asked Tony to introduce it. He did this beautifully, on a lovely summer evening in Winchester College. It seemed particularly apt that he was by then on the Governing Body of the College and is now President of Trinity, Oxford, both Dicky's places of education. I sent the journal and a synopsis of the story to Tony and asked him, were it to be published, if he would feel able to write a foreword. He replied that he would be 'honoured and delighted', and the result, when it arrived, surprised me very much indeed. Not only was he praising the journal, he was saying the most unexpected things about Simon, whom he had known, at intervals, for all his (Simon's) life.

Tony has a remarkable gift of words, not surprising for a philosopher, and this, coupled with his acute observation of character, which is never unkind, gave his writing of Simon an authenticity that aroused my curiosity. If Tony saw Simon in this way, what about all his other friends? I began to see the book in terms of a quest for a character, an exercise in piecing together a personality through the eyes of those who had known him. Most mothers, I hope, love their sons; but if they have any sense they know they are biased. I can very clearly admit that there were many things about Simon which could be — were — infuriating to others: anxious people felt threatened by his complete lack of anxiety which seemed foolhardy, and their reaction was of disapproval and condemnation. I saw several examples of that, always from those whose lack of confidence resulted in an obsessive attention to detail. But I loved him as he was, and I don't expect anyone to be interested in what I have to say about his character. I decided to tell his story as much as possible through the perceptions of his friends, and in doing so to learn more about the person with whom I had been so closely connected for 25 years.

We don't much discuss our children with other people, I think, any more than we discuss our husbands or wives. Or only superficially, never critically or analytically, and our friends seldom tell us what they really think of them. A pity, because we should learn a lot, as I found to my pleasant surprise when I embarked on this exercise. I knew that if I could persuade those who really knew Simon well to talk about him, warts and all, I might be on my way to finding out what he was like at heart, what sort of person he really was. Having seen how John Mead set about producing a documentary film about Tilman, I thought my plan should be to tape-record talks with those whose contributions I wanted, and build up a dossier of real evidence, which would be more convincing than hearsay, but in fact that didn't work, for two reasons: it made the finished script too disjointed, and there are few people so coherent and articulate that one can with pleasure read their speech. I have therefore had to produce the content of what was said as honestly as possible, rather like taking notes of evidence, never using a key word unless it was actually spoken.

The first people I thought of were the Johnsons. Michael Johnson was our doctor for many years. He came to Stockbridge at the end of 1950 with his wife Jean, and Mark, Clare, Stephen and Hal were born here. Mark was ten months older than Simon; they grew up together and when the time came they died together. During the most testing time, when *En Avant* was missing, Michael and Jean were the greatest help to me because we shared all the decisions that had to be made, and without them I would have felt unbearably alone. They are both practical, logical people and we could discuss everything realistically. I was very grateful to them.

They had suffered a terrible tragedy with Stephen's death at the age of fifteen in a shooting accident. It happened on the day that Mark and Stephen came home for the summer holidays, Mark's last day at Allhallows School. Michael had promised to take the two boys rook shooting after his evening surgery. Clare had just learnt to drive and she took them all up the hill to the belt of trees where the rooks congregated. She and Michael were arranging the return journey when they heard a shot and Mark's cry from the other side of the trees. Michael ran to find that Stephen had slipped and discharged his gun in falling. He died in the ambulance on the way to Winchester Hospital.

Mark and Simon, being much of an age, were natural companions. They went to their first school together, played with their trains in the Johnsons' attics, built boats to sail in the river here, were each included in the other family's outings. As soon as they were old enough to look for adventure alone they went off camping on a farm in Devon, catching fish in the Little Dart to fry over their camp stove. Boarding schools parted them, but it made no difference, and when the holidays came they were as usual in one another's houses. I don't remember them ever quarrelling or ever arguing, it seemed almost as if they were of one mind. Mark grew into a most attractive young man, and I think of him now with great joy. Although he never called me anything but Mrs Richardson (although Simon, when he grew up, called Jean Jean) I was not aware of a generation gap, mainly I think because he always struck me as mature. His sensitivity to other people was remarkable, and much heightened by the shock of Stephen's death. There was great strength in his gentle manner, and I loved him very much. When I think of him and Simon together I often find myself saying in my mind the lament — no, the song of rites for the dead — from *Cymbeline*, because they were certainly golden lads. Mark, like Simon, wanted to spend his life at sea and joined the Merchant Navy training school at Warsash in 1972. By 1977 he was a Second Officer, a navigator.

Michael remembers Simon being interested in mechanical things from a very early age, but not at all caring about playing games: he couldn't see any point in them, and if there was no point in doing something why bother? With characteristic dry realism, Michael remembers Simon tormenting their goat, Pansy, and the general delight when she broke her tether and chased him; the complaints from the local river keepers of the two boys' illegal exploits, to which he diplomatically didn't listen; Simon's independence at a very early age, hitch-hiking to join the family at their holiday home in Padstow, always welcome. (After Stephen's death the Johnsons all went down there, and Jean, sitting on the beach one day was amazed to see Simon walk out of the sea in front of her. A hitch had taken him to Rock, on the other side of the estuary, so he stripped off, tied his clothes in a bag on his head, and swam across the treacherous current to be with them.) And he remembers Simon's stoicism after the accident in

Scotland and his philosophical acceptance of the potentially very bad ankle which could have given him a lot of trouble in later life. 'I always thought of Simon as a quiet boy, he didn't make conversation for the sake of it, and he didn't say anything that wasn't worth saying. I'm sure he didn't suffer fools gladly, but I've never known him to say anything unkind about anybody. I have very many happy memories of him, especially during our holidays in Cornwall, fishing in the boat with me, when he often proved me wrong in my advice about bait and so on, and finally leaving Southampton in *En Avant*, of which he was extremely proud.'

Jean's story of Simon swimming across the Camel Estuary, which I had not heard before, was no surprise to me. Simon had no fear of the sea, it was his element. Dicky's friend, Paddy Tritton, with whom he had served in minesweepers during his time in the R.N.V.R., in the war, had a Gauntlet class yacht built by the Berthon Boat Company in Lymington. Paddy enjoyed teaching the young and helping them in every way, and as soon as Simon was old enough Paddy would take him sailing, sometimes just with Dicky, sometimes we all went. I remember once when Simon was eight or nine we were coming back from Lymington to Gosport in what seemed to me about a Force 6 gale, with Simon at the helm hardly able to hold her into the wind. The two men were standing down in the cockpit deep in conversation, and one or other from time to time would say over his shoulder, 'Keep her up, boy, keep her up.' I didn't dare to help Simon, but I sat below him so that he could brace his foot against my back and I could transfer some pressure to him. He was laughing with excitement at being able to hold the boat against the heavy sea. When years later he said — à propos of what I don't remember — 'You've always been very helpful to me, Mother', I thought of that moment and could feel again the pressure of his foot on my shoulder.

Simon went to Winchester College, to Beloes and Podge Brodhurst, and managed, not without some shaky times, to do reasonably well in his science A-levels. This surprised his dons, I think, because it was generally felt that he was incapable of writing anything coherently. The beauty of the buildings and their surroundings had a profound and lasting effect on him. Years later we were driving back late one night from Southampton, and as we came to the city limits he asked me if I had ever seen St Cross by moonlight. I hadn't, so he slewed the car off the road into the lane leading to the mediaeval almshouses and the Norman church. We walked across the

river to a seat on the far bank and sat in the moonlight for some time
without speaking; then Simon got up and I followed him back to the
car. I asked if he had done that often, and he said that he always went
down on the night of the full moon. He added that when he walked
from the college into the town he used to go through the Cathedral
because it was so beautiful. This was, of course, before the days of
the guardians with their collecting boxes.

During Simon's time at Winchester an exciting opportunity was
offered to him by his godfather, Bertie Blount, who had known
Dicky since they were at Trinity together. Bertie was retiring early
and planned a journey from the mouth of the Amazon to its source.
Simon was just sixteen and between exams, so Podge let him off a
week before the end of Short Half, that is the Christmas Term, and
Simon flew out to meet Bertie in Manaos. They did the trip up the
Amazon, over the Andes to Lima, to Cuzco and Machu Picchu,
across Lake Titicaca and home from La Paz. Simon arrived back the
day the next term started, looking like a ruffian with an enormous
machete in his hand, just in time to get his hair cut before he was due
back. His only regret was that the flight before his was hijacked to
Venezuela.

Henry Thompson, who I think helped Simon to become literate,
has a clear memory of him 'sitting at the back of the div., never
suffering fools gladly (his div. don included) impatient of banality in
discussions, bored by the ordinary grind of the classroom but
responsive to the unconventional — and hence not successful by
conventional classroom standards. He was very much his own man.'

When Simon left the school his housemaster, Geoffrey Hewitson
by now, expressed regret in his report that he was leaving and could
no longer keep the domestic machines in working order. (Please, Sir,
can Richardson come up to House at once, the washing machine is
flooding.) With adequate A-levels he got a place at Queen Mary
College to read civil engineering, which he did for a year, but he was
too impatient to get into the world and start living his life and he left.
He joined an organization that provided crews to deliver boats
anywhere in the world, and did several long-distance trips. At one
point he met a man who was building a concrete boat to enter the
Round the World race, and went to Preston to work on it for some
mo..ths. After that I think the owner's money ran out and Simon
went back to sea. He crewed a boat out to Athens, another back to
Porto Ercole on the west coast of Italy about a hundred miles north

of Rome, and was hanging about there hoping to get another boat back home when he met Alan Cowley.

Alan Cowley was a builder from Tunbridge Wells who had sold up and bought an old German E boat on which he was living with his young wife, Sara, and six-month-old Emma. He had noticed Simon sleeping on the quay, and after several very cold nights he felt sorry for him and invited him on board. Simon asked if there was any work he could do for Alan in return for his keep; so Alan, being at that time quite disillusioned with the young, gave him the least attractive job he could think of, cleaning the engine-room floor. It was checker-plate aluminium with years of grease and dirt trodden in. To his surprise, Simon took out every plate, cleaned it meticulously and put it back as new. They spent the days working together and the nights putting the world to rights, and when, after about three weeks, a Frenchman turned up who was looking for someone to help him take his boat back to Bordeaux through the canals, Alan was sorry to see Simon go. 'We never had a difference, we saw eye to eye on a great many things. I realize now that was not necessarily so, it was just Simon's nature which was like that, if he felt contented with a situation he let things go. I don't mean that he was easy going exactly, when opposition presented itself Simon was never nasty or rude, but absolutely adamant, and he could not be argued down. At the time I thought it was that we saw eye to eye, later I realized that because he was contented he saw no reason to disagree. He accepted what was pleasant about a situation and enjoyed it.'

Soon after that the Cowleys sold the boat and moved to Holland, where they bought a Dutch barge called *Johanna* from an elderly Dutchman called Cornelius Leunis — who later also proved very helpful to Simon — and set about converting it as a family home. Alan soon found that he needed a new generator, and, as the exchange was bad, he thought he would do better to buy it in England. He sent Simon the name of a firm near Oxford that he thought might have a re-conditioned one and asked Simon to negotiate for him, which he did, and took it out to Holland.

Paddy Tritton was a very dear friend. My one regret is that he has not lived to see this book published. Dicky was his First Lieutenant from 1941–44 and from then on Paddy was our great family friend. I shall never cease to be grateful for all the love he gave to the children, and for his friendship. He was a hard taskmaster to the young, and praise from him was real praise. By the time I had begun to ask those who knew Simon well for insights into his character Paddy was already into his last illness, and I felt it would be too great a strain to talk to him of Simon, whom he loved; but when he heard what I was up to, he told me that he had already written what he thought of Simon, and asked the nurse to bring a photostat copy of a document from his desk. This turned out to be a reference which Paddy had given the British Antarctic Survey in 1973, when Simon was trying to find ways of getting to the Antarctic and had written for a job. Paddy was most insistent that I should include it, and I must say that it is one of the most interesting things I have seen. It consists of twenty searching questions on the character and habits of an applicant for a two year stint in the remote areas of the Survey's work. The referee was asked to indicate marks from one to five in assessing the qualities needed. Paddy had answered by ringing either five or four, half of each. In the first group: he could be counted on to work long hours under adverse conditions, he is completely reliable and responsible, he is well liked by his associates, and [even] he is personally clean and tidy — which may have been true at the time, but after *En Avant* was bought, clean would not have applied — he is stable and well-adjusted, in restricted living conditions he would not be a source of friction, he is a willing subordinate when the situation requires, he has no distasteful personal characteristics, and I would select him to work and live with under adverse field conditions. In the blank section under Additional Remarks, Paddy had written 'Whatever Simon takes on he will do well. He has an inventive mind and a fair share of imagination. Above all, he has a great sense of humour.'

This is dated 16 February 1973. Whether or not the British Antarctic Survey would have offered Simon a job I don't know, because very shortly after this something much more exciting turned up. In answer to an advertisement in *The Times*, which turned out to be from Merton Naydler, a London solicitor, Simon was passed on to the legendary H. W. Tilman who was looking for crew for his yacht *Baroque* for a voyage to the west coast of Greenland and into the Arctic Circle. At Queen Mary College Simon had taken up climbing and joined several climbs with the club. He had heard of Major Tilman and read everything he could find by him and about him. The combination of climber, sailor, author and philosopher held a powerful attraction, and when Simon was invited to go down to Mylor, near Falmouth, he jumped at the chance. The story of that meeting, and of the subsequent voyage, is told by Tilman in his book *Ice with Everything*. Simon, unbeknownst to me, was also keeping a journal and the two, taken together are most interesting.

It is also interesting to read, in *Ice with Everything*, that Tilman found that he 'had picked a winner in Simon Richardson, active, energetic, knowledgeable about boats and engines, and a thorough seaman so far as an amateur sailor can attain to that honourable title.' And he ended his account of the voyage to Greenland:

> In climbing mountains or sailing the seas one often has to settle for less than one hoped. Instead of Ellesmere Island we had to settle for Greenland, and considering the short time we had to prepare her for a hard voyage she did well to get us there and the crew did well to get her back. In theory the skipper of a small boat should be able to do rather better than his crew anything that is required either on deck or aloft. With the handicap of age more had to be left to the crew and I was thankful to have Simon, active and competent, backed up by the others who were equally active if less competent. More important, however, is for them to have the right outlook. Activity can be instilled and competence can be acquired, but the right attitude must be ingrained — the cheerful acceptance and endurance of small privations and wearisome duties and the unquestioned belief that the success of the voyage and the care of the ship is what matters most. 'This ship, the ship we serve, is the moral symbol of our life.'

THE VOYAGE TO GREENLAND WITH
H. W. TILMAN IN 1973

SIMON RICHARDSON'S JOURNAL

THE OLD MAN is definitely unhappy at the moment. We came here to Cork for John Harradine, the guy who said he has toothache, which I don't believe, who has cleared off. He was very keen four months ago, but didn't appear at Mylor until two days before we left. When he did arrive he came with a useless American called Steve who hadn't a clue about sailing or much else. We hang around waiting, not being able to get away, with another guy from Mylor who has just telegraphed saying sorry he can't come. No doubt someone will turn up sometime, but we won't be able to get as far north as we wanted. It doesn't worry me too much, but time gets shorter and shorter.

Our journey from Mylor was uneventful, except that Ilan was seasick and also John, who was expected to be the one who wouldn't be. I have been trying to take good photos. We are now becalmed a hundred miles south of Ireland starting the long slog of making our westing and northing — more sleeps in the afternoon today and we search round for things to do. I had to go up the mast this morning to swop round a halyard that was chaffing off on something, while we were wallowing around — most uncomfortable — I should have taken my camera up with this fast film in but hanging on was a great problem, and uncomfortable. We have just had the tiller off to tighten up a few of the bolts that have worked loose. They will do so again and next time we will probably leave them to come off. The bolts holding the tiller to the stock were easy to take out but not to put back and in the end we had to bond them so they are now pre-stressed and to my liking — the threads are somewhat buggered up, but that's of no import.

The new guy, Jonno Barrett, who finally arrived at Cork, is nineteen or thereabouts. Good school, thinks he knows the lot but doesn't — quite a lot but not everything — he has brought the modern classics to keep him going; *First Circle*, *Ulysses*, *Clayhanger* etc., while I struggle on with the *Decameron* and Brian with the *1001 Nights*, very enjoyable and better than Chaucer anyday, 'a kissed mouth doesn't lose its freshness, for like the moon it always renews itself. I think of you all a lot and dream too of the best of you.'

This is a very curious life I lead at the moment. The Old Man hangs off us all like a magnet. We all respect him no end, though he does some of the most curious things but still keeps us amused. I am blamed for losing the marlin spike that hangs on the mast, for which I receive the rhetoric, 'Fortunately, or unfortunately, I don't like marlin spikes. This is the last thing of use we have' — to be followed moments later by, 'If it works, then it's obsolete.' The spike was found later in its proper place. A tanker has just been sighted. What they think we are doing I can't imagine.

We have just spent an amusing half hour getting up the storm jib, in the whole of Force 6. It looks like half a pocket handkerchief and most of the stitching has broken up already. What it would be like in a gale I can't imagine. She behaves like a bitch with a big sea on the beam but very quiet elsewhere. We take in 100 gallons an hour occasionally and it has been my job to clear the shit out of the pumps. We are all getting used to the appalling wet that pervades everywhere. The semi-rotary is simple, but the whale pump seems to produce pressure build-ups in some extraordinary way, and then when you release the outlet valve and close it up again it works like a charm for a few minutes — repeat as necessary. A most impractical way to travel. The winds are predominantly N.W., exactly the way we are going. I know in two weeks time I shall be sick of seeing N.W. always 45 degrees off. It's frustrating already.

We have just had this fair wind from the S.W. and within six hours of it arriving we have had to reduce sail so much that we are now not moving at all, just rolling around everywhere with water pouring all over the saloon floor. It clears it up I suppose but we got porridge all over my bunk and belongings. All good clean fun and it's a fantastic change from steaming round the Mediterranean. We have been seeing many a Wilson's or Stormy Petrel, lovely little black birds with swept-back wings a foot across. I caught a gannet with a long yellow beak, brilliant blue eyes and yellow head. My fishing rod suddenly went double and we had this enormous bird on the end. I put on leather gloves and coat and we hauled him in, when very near he got quite ferocious and attacked the log line in my hand and I was most worried for my face. However, once aboard he was quite passive and

didn't flap at all while he was being photographed. We then heaved
him overboard and he took about a minute to take off, much to our
concern. The next thing that was sighted half an hour later was a vast
tail fin, a smaller pectoral fin and no dorsal. This huge unidentifiable
fish swum on the surface about 50 feet away for a minute or two and
then disappeared slowly. We reckoned that he was about four or five
feet long. Following this excitement, about half an hour later there
was another large fin sighted on the bow apparently stationary. It
turned out to be a Dan buoy — we think — but unfortunately owing
to an almost total calm we could not reach the thing. The skipper says
that he found one like this with 200 feet of good two-inch rope
attached in the Davis Strait; we weren't allowed to use the engine or
anything to go and find it, all very well, but half a mile of rope would
be very useful to us.

Yet another problem, this time greater than the rest he sets us. The
chain plates on the port side have given way. They have pulled away
from the frames and have pulled up one of the planks. There is a gap of
about an inch in the loo where broad daylight pours in on the port
tack. It was most dispiriting indeed to turn S.E. back to civilisation, if
you could call it that. We aimed for Bantry Bay, being very lucky with
the winds to keep us on the starboard tack all the way in till we hove to
in a thick fog just outside — a frightening experience off the west coast
of Ireland in a poor boat, not knowing where you were. At one stage
during the night all the lights showed up, putting us about six miles
S.S.E. of this great headland Bull Head. Next time we saw any lights
we were about a mile away. We motored into Castletown, a most
precarious place to enter even in broad daylight, anchored and found
the Harbour Master, it being a Sunday. We had a brief look round the
place, so Irish as to be unbelievable, cows in the main square,
MacFlaerty's Bar, O'Neill's Bar, bog isn't the word for it, it's all so
primitive. There are many fishing boats, and this one small yard on
Bear Island. Yes, we've been to Bear Island. This guy, Murphy will be
his name for sure, has his yard where there was an old naval base,
Napoleonic. We could hardly get the boat to turn all the corners to get
her here. He has an arc welder and power tools so we should be out in a
couple of days if luck permits. There is a French sailing school and four
houses, including the bar-cum-grocery shop, a few rotten old cars and
a telegraph tower on top of the hill. I hope to be able to get out for a
day in the gloom and the mist and the fog to find some mussels. It's all

too romantic for me. I am imagining myself wandering around with some girl, not talking much, just listening to the cows and the waves. I suppose I have just been at sea too long. To cap it all, having just finished the *Decameron* I am starting out on *Ulysses* — so appropriate as we are in an old naval fortress on the west coast of Ireland.

We had a seagull on board a few days ago. It flew into the rigging and collapsed on deck and staggered around for a few minutes and then heaved itself overboard and just managed to make the air again. We might get some seagulls' eggs. We saw an eyot of theirs on the way in so we can combine it with the mussel collecting expedition, if time allows. We might, if we are even luckier, dry some of our clothes but the mist has not lifted for 24 hours. I'm now thinking of Corsica where I slept out on the beach and all was always absolutely dry. A place I must go back to. I met good people there, the two Dutch couples, the mad American, the Italian girl and the two sets of two English girls. The countryside stark and unyielding, like my letter writing, which I must do soon to keep people happy, everybody expects a letter or postcard. It seems pointless writing letters even if there was time.

We are frantic to get on from here. Third time lucky, and there will never be time to write on our way to Greenland; when we are in the ice will be the time and then no doubt we will be back before the letters. An Irishman who didn't introduce himself has just stepped aboard with his young son at 9.45 p.m. and asked to have a look round. He is the ferryman, shopkeeper, farmer, daytrip man with a finger in everything. Lawrence Cove, where we are anchored now, is totally sheltered and there is hardly room to swing a boat. Two boats our size could not possibly get in, let alone anchor here. The entrance of Castletown is easy compared with this. As we cannot turn to port when going slowly we nearly landed on the rocks, but getting out will be easier. The materials to do the chain plates have not yet arrived from Cork but we can get on and do the patching up of the frames today, and find a large plank of oak to fit under the stringer to spread the load right along from the loo porthole to the forward end of the galley.

Today is the 21st of June. We've been here for four days trying to get ourselves ready. I have fitted a vast piece of Honduras teak in position and have drilled all the holes out. It is now a question of fitting all the pieces back together again, welding bits here and there and filing out all the holes for the bolts to fit in. The bolts are five-eighths as opposed to the original half-inch, and instead of three we have five, and another two of half an inch. This gives us the equivalent of three times as many as we had before. If that lot gives I shall go home. The caulking will take time, and putting the galley back together and all. We should be here for less than a week anyway. Today was Corpus Christi so everyone was on holiday — not that Murphy (Finbar, would you believe it?) is doing much. One of his lads did two hours work and another did one, drilling a few holes in the chain plates.

The Old Man blew his top at Jonno yesterday evening. 'Don't call me Major, I'm not in the bloody army now.' Ilan, the cook, is hungry again and it's only 9.30 p.m. He has a complicated way with eggs of putting them into boiling water and leaving them off the heat hoping they will cook just right. They never get beyond the runny stage, as is logical. When Brian McClanaghan said 'Not fucking runny eggs again' the Old Man looked rather alarmed. Ilan cooks well but there is not really enough for my demanding stomach.

It is now a quarter to eight of the next morning. We had gone over to the pub at about 9.30 last night and we were invited back by the man who dives and seems to be doing some sort of research here — marine biology — and there was singing and dancing till three with the people from the French sailing school from Concarneau. They were all nice people. Jonno got stoned out of his mind and so we were left trying to get a boat to go across in. Not only was it low tide, it was the lowest tide I have ever seen here, so we floundered around in the mud a little and then went off to the sailing centre, found a bed and slept. Ilan found himself in the girls' dormitory when he was woken at 7.15 this morning. The skipper was very surprised to see me up and running around as usual. Yet another day passes and still all is not finished, but tomorrow should see us through with luck.

Today is the longest day and we have finished. All the bolts are in except three small buggers which hold the metal straps in right at the bottom. We might need Donald, the fair haired, bearded 28-year-old marine biologist, to come and give us a hand with all his diving gear. The galley has to be done and I am being awakened at first light by the skipper tomorrow. I said I would do the galley tonight and the three bolts tomorrow morning, and he said that there would be no problem waking me at dawn. We had four dozen mussels each tonight with lashings of garlic and spring onions, followed by a duff and a lot of bullshit from our learned friend the boy about paintbrushes. He now never stops talking and drives us slowly round the bend. It will be great to be back at sea where we do not have to talk to each other if we don't want to. He really enjoys being up the mast though, which should relieve me of one job. It was such a relief when the last and outer bolt of the chain plate went in. It has been a slow day aligning everything into perspective. I went for the old unofficial swim just before the mussels to see if I could get this beastly bolt in — no luck — and called it a day about midnight. I was woken, rudely, at 5 a.m. by Ilan, and by breakfast we had a good start on the job expecting Donald to come and dive to put the bolt back in. At 9 a.m. he arrived just as the skipper shits in his face, which did not help. Two more bolts were drawn to find that they were so corroded it is not believable, also when one is bolted in half the frame disintegrates as it is only made of pitch, so at 11 a.m. with water everywhere Finbar is called in and decrees, very rightly, that all the bolts below the waterline on the side with the steel plates should be checked, so, in the half dark, at the top of the tide at 10 p.m., we shift her, nearly driving into some of the dinghies moored out near us. I must say I admire the Old Man's judgement in allowing for distances. I was convinced we would run into one, but no — about a foot clearance. I don't understand how he does it, or is it just luck that stops him destroying his boats more often?

Jonno is getting on the skipper's nerves like mad at the moment. When he was doing the washing-up after supper the old boy said 'Why all the song and dance about it, just get on and do it.' At any rate, the galley above the sink is all in place, reasonably firmly, but no doubt it will all come out again in a few days' time. We should at the present rate of striking get away on Tuesday morning at midday if all goes well tomorrow. We have just finished mooring at 12.30 p.m. having started at 10, most of it in the dark not knowing what's happening anywhere. A total waste of effort so late at night as no work can be done till 6 p.m. tomorrow when it is low tide again. I am worried that we shall sink into the mud too far during the night. The Old Man is not turning in yet so he is probably expecting to be up for another hour or two. I have been depressed all day, and I shouted vehemently at Brian this morning quite unjustifiably.

7.30. Breakfast at 7.30, ugh. The skipper is fed up with all of us or so it seems. He said 'We can get the big anchor up this morning,' and I pulled a face as if to suggest that it was going to be an amusing operation shifting a hundredweight of fisherman from under the bobstay, at which he snarled back 'You won't have to get your hands dirty because I washed it this morning.' Thought for the day: having just talked about the Archbishop of Canterbury and the Pope — 'Good old cocks, nice chaps to have a chat with.' I suppose that's what they're for, just amplified clergymen.

We have just had afternoon tea at exactly 4.30 waiting for the tide to go down so we can get a few remaining bolts back in and out. Perhaps we will leave at night though I hope not. It will mean tacking out of the bay with supertankers charging in at ten knots. The weather forecast is not good anyway, with either westerlies or northerlies four to six, not much good either way. We can hear it properly at 17.55 D.S.T.. We will be back on G.M.T. soon which makes the navigation easier although we will stay on it while we go further and further west so we will arrive in Greenland many hours out.

We leave at last: midday 16th June, and drift out with the tide. I have just finished the galley at 11.30, time for a glass of Guinness and off we go. It is a relief but no climax. The port side of the boat is now good and strong, and I hope will remain so. Jonno is getting on our nerves again. He says his back hurts and just stands around getting in the way telling everybody what to do. Last night he said 'I'm sorry to be so boring' at which we all said 'Good heavens, you're not boring,' and 'What, you boring?' and so on, but the Old Man had this great grin from ear to ear.

A quiet wind pushes us on our way, N.W. by W. It's great to be heading in the right direction again, gaining our westing and northing in this way till we hit Cape Farewell. It used to be called Cape Desolation, not an appropriate name for our landfall, if landfall we make it. Last night we did a remarkable five knots to windward. Curious that she should move so well. I spend a lot of my time letting the jib further out to stop it backing the foresail and someone, I think the Old Man, just pulls it in again. Brian, Ilan and I have lengthy discussions on matters of no importance, we chop and change to start with and then settle down, about half an hour later, on some masterly cultural subject which I usually know nothing about, so I listen carefully and break in occasionally with some totally inappropriate remark.

June 27th, another fine day, Solent sailing weather. The sun shines but there is a cool wind, and we tool along at two knots with a few old timbers groaning in the rigging, the slop of water in tanks, and the gentle flowing past as the new chain plates, extended to the water line, dip below the water. We have just hauled in a dozen mackerel with Ilan's feathers being far more effective than my spinner. I have just been told that I should have my head examined for reading Joyce's *Ulysses* — the Old Man thinks it is all smut and about a man having a shit. I can't understand most of it, rather like the Bible, but I enjoy the language and having spent a week in the exact sort of countryside I get a small feeling for what this man is trying to put across. I have just read that last paragraph and the ideas are terribly disjointed. I think of something for a minute or two, try to put it down on paper, and forget ·all I wanted to say. If I go on like this every day, perhaps in a month or two I could train myself to stop longer on an idea, expand and expound, and then put some ideas on paper. I hope at the end of this voyage to write a page or two on the Old Man, a sketch would be good.

The wind has come at last S.W.S., almost perfect if we don't reduce the headsail too much. The port chainplates are O.K., but we are taking water high up by the forward chainplate on the starboard side. I think we will get trouble from that quarter before our days are out. We are careening along at about four to five knots with the wind on our beam, twenty days of this and we could be there, about eleven hundred miles to Cape Farewell. We take air and sea temperatures and cloud formation. I am intending to make up a few graphs of wind force and direction, sea and air temperatures and position, with graphs of sea/position; sea/force and direction; air/sea; air/force and direct-ion. We might get some interesting plots somewhere along these lines. Today's position is 51.54 N. 13.20 W.

From my bunk I can look up through a skylight and see the mast and sails. This has a curiously limiting factor, it depends what tacks we are on. On port tack I must sleep with head forward so the drips land on my feet, and on starboard with head aft so drips land on my feet. The leaks come in just below the two portholes in the saloon where the deck hits the coach-roof. I can't exactly see why, but I shall try and caulk it one of these days.

During the midnight and graveyard watches I go through my hundred foot imaginary yacht surveying everything, making rules to be broken and making everything as simple as possible, the more I think about it the more I realise how easy it is to make things. This chainplate business was a great enlightener how to build things strong enough in wooden boats. It's not a proposition I would ever contemplate starting, building in wood from scratch, but using healthy steel materials to replace wooden ones is a must as long as you do not cover too much of the wood and stop the air getting in. It is now the cook's watch, and I must stop to catch up with last night's awakedness, I'll manage another few pages of *Ulysses* but I don't think I will ever finish it and will no doubt start on *Clayhanger* which even the skipper seems to like.

Another morning, another day. Still a fair wind, though precious little of it last night. We are on the port tack, so it is difficult to write with any modicum of literacy. I'm just pounding through *Most Secret* by Nevil Shute for the ninth time — it's still very good. At six this morning it was blowing Force 7 on the beam, and we were hanging on comfortably enough, but making water at a prodigious rate, when the skipper came up saying the weather forecast was Force 8 in all west coast areas with severe gales in our own. We became a little frantic about this. It immediately started moderating and veered to the west as per forecast, so we hove to for supper. At ten the sky is clear, the sun shines, but it is filthy to windward so we stay hove to a little less comfortably than before. It is down to Force 6 steady. We are in a little less of a panic now, at least the skipper is. I suppose we must have a good Atlantic blow before our time is up. It might still be a long night, and we slow down, but with luck we might get a reasonable night's sleep. Our dear ship behaves very well in these conditions, she's dry above — reasonably — but wet below. There's one definite leak through the panelling above the skipper's bunk and I have just rigged yet another piece of canvas so that I can sleep the same end not dependent on which tack we are. I am up against my leeboard most of the time, which is comfortable except entry and exit from the drip-free end and the rushing of the bilge water across the saloon floor. The cheap sails are not wearing very well. The clew of the staysail pulled out the other day and I did a hasty repair which I have been meaning to do properly ever since. The one on the jib is about to go too, in as much as the round thimble has come out and is stuffed into my oily top which is all right while the rope holds, but it will not for long. The cringles in all four corners of the main do not look happy either. The stitching in all of them is appalling, only single stitching which will no doubt go one day, not like proper canvas, says the Old Man. It isn't, thank God. We had a bit of a fiasco this morning trying to get the creases out of the rolled material while going downwind, quite impossible if one thinks about it, but we did get the flaps out in some miraculous way.

Next morning we are still hove to as from 1800 hours last night. The wind has increased and varying from a steady Force 7 with an entry for my watch 53W. 78N. No doubt we will come across another gale that is worth writing about, all the same the seas are really mountainous and we crash into them on the leeward side with abandon. It is a curiously dry gale, rain squalls come every half hour or so and we pump like mad as she heels over to a steady thirty degrees. As far as we çan see most of the water comes in round the top plank on the starboard side. Luckily we do not have to do any of the steering, or else there would have to be someone to pump as well. I hope this leak is from only one spot, otherwise we might be in trouble.

Later I have located exactly the source of trouble, but we cannot put her about to do work on her. The Old Man has been up most of the night counting the lulls, but has not reached any conclusion about the time of abatement owing to the non-existence of his hearing aid. 'The first rise after the low will mean a harder blow' is a word of wisdom for the day. Yesterday's was 'When the sea jumps it is time to man your pumps.' The sky is clearing to windward with large cumulus clouds forming. The glass might be rising so perhaps we are nearing this depression's end. The glass has been down to 1002, but the depression 800 miles west of Rockall moving rapidly N.E. is 970 — a long way to go yet. The skipper is off getting his sights in his efficient manner with amazing alacrity and precision.

I feel really weak at 10 a.m. at the end of my watch. We pump, for about ten minutes an hour, about 200 gallons an hour — four bathfuls come in every hour — quite a thought that one new, yellow, cast alloy, £25 pump, and one old garden one, keep the boat between us and the deep blue sea. They are both working well now and the level is controllable, and not really very much, when you consider the actual volume we pump out in terms of jerry-cans full. I feel sorry flinging Ilan from his requisitioned bunk and dry sleeping-bag, but I feel I am about to crash myself, so must take over what is rightly mine.

Next watch, 6 to 8 p.m. Only a few squalls now and mostly down to Force 4. We will set sail after supper, which will be a change for the better. We will probably only make N.N.W., but it is better than far-reaching and only going to leeward or Lourdes. Having just finished the gin bottle, I wrote a 'Message to the World' Yacht *Baroque*,

estimated position, All Well, and my address, and threw it overboard.
I suppose it might get to someone, though I don't think there are many
sandy beaches on the west coast of Ireland where it can get washed up,
but it's all very romantic. Only about a hundred strokes on the pump
during the last hour, a great improvement.

[This message in the bottle was indeed washed up on the Fanore
Beach on the west coast of Ireland, and found by a ten-year-old boy on
holiday from Dublin who no doubt also thought it romantic, and it
was posted back home. Some correspondence followed — D.R.]

We have just had a reminiscence over John Harradine, the toothache
guy, and I recalled when the Old Man strode up with a pair of
steelsons in his hand and a menacing look on his face, which alarmed
John and I laughed, which he didn't appreciate.

Joyce interests me more and more. I suppose I will take to reading it
in bits, as I get pretty befuddled. The bulwark up forward has
disintegrated, new wood as well, just one section between the
stanchions. Also the rubbing-strake from whisper-stays forward has
all pulled away. This was new wood, and it has large screws every six
inches or so. Part of the dinghy lashings have also parted. That was not
so surprising as it was the rotten old log-line that would not have
served as a dog lead. I suppose we must repair that before it breaks
right away. I hope we can get on the starboard tack to bung up the hole
that has been giving all the trouble near the skipper's bunk.

The first of July, and we started to sail last night with a westerly wind,
and come this morning we are tooling along at a quiet 2–3 knots.
There is a vast accumulation of rain ahead which I hope we will miss,
but it would get the salt off my oilies if nothing else. They always say
in the instructions to wipe over with fresh water immediately after
use; where Mr Hansen thinks we would find it, I would not know.
Looking through the log last night I find that we have made 1,100
miles since leaving Falmouth. How much of that is made good I do
not like to think, but we are now out of B.B.C. forecasting range,
somewhere just N.N.W. of the Shannon-Rockall line. The rain squall
is getting nearer but I think we will miss it. 'When the wind is from the
north with a dropping barometer, beware.' The wind has just veered
and increased a little, time to tighten up the staysail.

Last night we had a bullshitting time from the skipper. We had been
up during all of the night before. Jonno and Brian started to put up the
canvas jib, the wrong one as it turned out, so not surprisingly it took

them an hour, the sail was totally unprepared for use. We had to take it down because the leech, or is it the luff, was stretched out of all recognition. Jonno was in a vile mood, cursing all and sundry, whereat the skipper told him not to touch anything in case he made a balls of it, to which Jonno replied in a la-de-da voice 'Sarcasm, I have always been told, is the lowest form of wit.'

As I watch the bowsprit it moves around madly in all directions. I was convinced it was going to give last night when we had this curious jib up, that I think had been used as a storm kreel or some such. When this thing filled, the bowsprit shook and the topmast shook. I have been for a visit up the mast to get the jib halyard strop off as it is chaffing against the mast. We then set to to repair the rubbing-strake and the bulwark, and I came to the simple conclusion that the rubbing-strake was better off off, and the bulwark as it is. I went over the side to get the remaining screws off, and got an unofficial dip into the bargain. In the end I took all my clothes off to save them getting wet and my backside got a good wash. We have now got a beam wind about Force 3, and are going under full sail — all very comfortable until we put the lee rail under and we have to start pumping again. It goes under at about 20 degrees heel when we start to reduce canvas. The temperature is going down, and once one's hands begin to feel the cold I think that is a good sign. We are all looking forward to getting into the ice. The idea that we won't now get to Ellesmere does not worry us, although we could still get there but we would have to turn back almost immediately. I am having difficulty now in writing. The other good sign is that one can still read at 11.30 B.S.T., and it gets light at about four. It will be great when there is only one night watch as such, though it will probably be very disorienting. The Old Man speaks more now if you prompt him. He talks of his time in Albania, and when he was stationed in Preston in 1915, and went to the Bull and Royal. This life is something of a change from Preston for him and for me.

I have been working out how much I would have to write to be able to produce a novel of say 60,000 words. Each page has about 600 words, a page a day, 100 days, about right. No one would buy it though. I will copy out the complete log to fill up space, also provisions. Ilan has a complete inventory of all we have eaten. My graphs will pad out some more. A full character sketch of each person, especially the Old Man. If I could put down some of my thoughts I would be happier, but this is a vast improvement on the zero. As for

my thoughts, they lie principally on what I have done and what I want
to do: my bare 120 foot steel yacht, capable of standing a winter or two
in pack ice, and laying over on her side for mechanical purposes
always hardy and efficient. When we get north of the Arctic Circle I
think things change as there will be so much that is so new — the
people and their way of life, the scenery and the cold.

The Old Man and I were talking of the N.W. Passage this
afternoon, and how he would like to do it and so would I. My watch
this evening was centred on me and my boat, taking three years, and
people like Tilman, Colin Putt and others, costs done and great
enjoyment. I suppose it could work one day. Apparently, Spitzbergen
has never been circumnavigated under sail and is therefore on my list.
At the end of my watch there was a rain squall followed by an
incredible rainbow. It became a double one and the inner one came
down to the transom. I've never seen it so near — so gold — coming
on what I had been planning it seemed like an omen but all it meant
was that a squall had just passed, very useful.

In the main saloon Brian, Ilan and I sleep. Lots of talk of what we
will do this year, next year, sometime. They are older, 28 years, and
don't have anything yet. Perhaps I will be like that, but I hope not. (As
a treat I have changed my socks to the second towelling ones,
noticeably warmer than the woollen ones.)

July 2nd, becalmed all morning, wallowing about, we got all the sails
down and I started on the leak by the starboard chainplates. I managed
to get a piece of canvas tacked on, at which it started raining. Then I
nailed the chopped off piece of rubbing-strake back and covered it in
Swedish putty and paint and gunge. It should be O.K. At lunchtime
the wind went right round to the east, and five hours later we are still
running at five knots in exactly the right direction, and let's hope it
stays for a week. As we were working on the leak an American jet flew
right overhead, circled, and came in at 50 feet about 40 yards away
twice, amazingly right out in the middle of the Atlantic. A pity they
could not drop us some fresh food or whatever, a bar of chocolate
perhaps. My chocolate is lasting well. I bought six bars of 10p stuff
and have one for every dark watch. There won't be one tonight, and
the last will go tomorrow night. We are now almost going fast enough
for the turbulence to start under the stern. The sea is delightfully calm
and we surge gently around the place. The tiller has started to play up
again; the locking washers and plug spanner and my razor-blade

wedge have had no effect. I am surprised at this and a little disappointed. It should last us out, and we have the emergency one if it just lifts off one day. I doubt if we will try a third time to repair it, as the bolts holding the tiller to the stock probably won't go back in as it is so difficult to align the holes when drilling — one must drill from both sides.

Do you know which opera sounds like a railway? The Rose of Castile. — Joyce — quite clever, I reckon. It is still raining and blowing up a bit. We are steaming along very happily. The signs are ominous; my sunrise entry in the log is of crimson streaks on a yellow background where the sun rose above the clouds; now the rain before the wind, a N.E. gale perhaps. We are obviously north of this certain depression that is working north-eastwards; very comfortable as long as it keeps its distance, though if it does not back we could make good use of it even if it did blow up. Ilan is ploughing his way through *The Magus*, another of those books that I did not finish last year in the sun. A book about the Ionian Islands would be good to re-read and finish when it gets cold. It is now a family joke, as he spends so much time reading it and never finishes.

5.30 p.m. Running at perhaps seven knots. Five days of this and we would be there — it's a great feeling to be really moving again, and not plunging into the seas at about five points in the wind. Let's hope it lasts two, perhaps three days; very lucky. We will probably take a reef in tonight before dark. Have just built my cocoon up ever further, it should now keep me dry and warm and sweaty. It is only glued halfway along, and does not meet the canvas square that is tacked on over my head to keep the drips off that. How long the polythene will last I do not know. The skipper has the best method of attacking at source: he makes drainpipes that run along underneath the beam, but he still gets wet all the time, but it does not seem to worry him. He wears the same clothes day in, day out, and does not have any others — perhaps he'll put another sweater underneath the one which has *Baroque* knitted into it, given to him by his sister (I think).

From the galley comes the hiss of the pressure cooker as we roll. Ilan sits on his bumrest singing blues noisily to himself. He seems very content to produce our food even after all our snide comments, although we could do with a little more first course and less duff, which we get twice a week: steamed puddings, like we used to get at school, but they are sometimes better, and sometimes only hot dough. I think he forgets to put the baking powder in. Brian, who I think could be termed in Edward Wilson's words as 'a good brick' is hopelessly engaged, involved with *The Magus*. The minute Ilan put it down he picked it up and has read about half of it already. The wind still bears down on us. I have the same feeling as the square riggers must have had after endless months of beating full and bye, suddenly, after a day of calm, to pick up the Trade Winds, soon to be changed to the Cape Horn sails. Speaking of the cook, I smell prunes — luckily I have persuaded him not to put them in the curry. Swan Vestas matches, though really good on shore, are terrible at sea; the sandpaper just decays when the slightest bit damp.

Tuesday, 3rd July — Becalmed yet again. The wind backed all the night and by dawn this morning we were close hauled. By 9 we were totally becalmed. The sun is out and almost hot. I don't understand all these calms. It seems ridiculous to be stuck out in the middle of the Atlantic with the barometer going up and up. No doubt tomorrow it will be blowing a gale. I expect there is a vast high pressure area to the south of us giving us gentle useless N.W. winds. We have nearly two points of verification with us at the moment — no help one way or the other — the wind will still blow in the direction that it wants to. I am looking forward to running back already. I sit on the counter with my rucksack frame as the backrest. It makes all the difference not to have that sharp chunk of wood that digs in somewhere. We are moving but the log does not turn. Occasionally it will give half a turn the right way and half a turn back a minute later. I was up the mast yet again this morning to replace the strop that holds up the jib halyard. A simple operation, except that with the boat rolling all over the place, I needed all my time and trouble to hold on. A calm sea with a fair amount of wind is the best condition for the ascent, as the shrouds are taut and not flapping wildly. The jump from the top of the shrouds to the cross-trees is a precarious one, as I am always hooked on to something — usually a halyard.

16.30 Engine started. We will probably run for an hour, when the Old Man will be fed up with the noise, smell, vibration and fog of diesel fumes. The port 50-gallon oil-drum tank leaks through the air pipe as we heel, and drips on to the asbestos coating of the exhaust, so every time she's started the whole boat fills up with diesel fumes till it has all been evaporated from the pipe. Luckily we kept all the sails up as there was just enough wind from the west to stop them flapping madly. The poor helmsman, me at the moment, receives all the exhaust in his face as the exhaust pipe is led up through the deck, up the side of the dog-house and into his face — very inebriating. We do about five knots at 1,800 revs, and I suppose she would do about seven if pushed up to 2,400, although the boat would probably fall to pieces in the process. She won't turn to port at all at slow speeds, as the prop is way out on that side, so manoeuvring is very very difficult. At speed she'll run about all over the place — we stuck it for an hour. It did produce some wind, about four knots from the south west, I suppose it could lead to greater things.

I have just been reading the basic introduction of the *Arctic Pilot*. It paints a very glum picture of gales, paths of depression, freezing cold, adverse currents, winds, calms. Massive amounts of ice everywhere — a couple of pages on tropical revolving storms etc. Our calm still stays, it will be 12 hours soon. So tedious when we are so far behind time; at the present rate we will not be in Greenland till August. We will get to Greenland though by hook or by crook. The latest plan is to make for Umanak, at about 70 N. — quite far enough I suppose to have my essentials frozen blue.

A light southerly wind helps us on our way. Long may it remain, anyway for all the night I hope. We go back to G.M.T. tonight, which means an extra half hour for Jonno and me. I tried to explain to the skipper that instead of doing half an hour more we could make it much easier and do half an hour less each and do half of one watch twice. He didn't get it. He has been a little frightened by my barograph takeoff. I have been keeping a graph of pressure/time. One can get a much better idea of what is happening by seeing it in pictorial terms, rather than a whole lot of consecutive numbers. The skipper has just told me of a story of a sperm whaler that went on voyage for three years. The captain never went to civilised places because he assumed the crew would mutiny!!!

I have been talking to the skipper a lot lately during his watches. He enjoys himself when talking to one person, but with a crowd he retreats into his shell a little. We were talking of his expeditions to the Antarctic and how he would like to have another go at Smith Island — somewhere south of the Shetlands. The only thing that seems to stop him is the lack of reliable crew, and the difficulty of finding people who would be prepared to go down there for a year and spend 83 days at sea. He was also telling me of an expedition just before the war to the Himalaya that cost them £300 each. Cargo boat to Calcutta £30, 3 Sherpas £10 a month. It's a pity that people of today have to mount a vast expedition raising thousands of pounds as opposed to quietly sailing off not telling anyone, like the Old Man. Apparently he appeared at one of the British bases in the Shetlands to be completely shunned by the people there — not asked to their hut or anything, all because he had not notified them that he was going to be in that part of the world — as if the British owned the place. Any foreign base would be delighted to see you, and give you all the help and assistance you wanted or asked for.

I must say it would be fantastic to set off in a boat down there. I reckon I could dig up a crew who would really be prepared to go and like it. Tilman hates the bother of doing something like this, and therefore cannot choose the best as opposed to taking the dregs. John, although a pleasant sort of guy, is impatient whereas Ilan, Brian and I can let the little worries pass over. Brian, although having been before, knows very little of any technical aspects of the thing, and Ilan does not have a clue but just enjoys himself. In a way, I am spoiling myself by coming on this trip — even now I have absolutely no regrets about giving up University. This life to me seems ideal — so down to earth but beautifully and aesthetically so. I now wonder why I was so thrilled about going round the world in the first place. No doubt my next boat, if next there be, will be a great anticlimax. One's ideas, standards, hopes change all the time as one becomes more aware of what one enjoys and needs. I must really get on and find out what this celestial navigation is all about. It must be simple if the skipper can do it so effectively. Years of experience, mind you. Seeing him do an eye-splice is invigorating — although he seems to have difficulty in doing it, he produces something beautiful and entirely efficient.

Wednesday 4th July — All night we carried the force three S.S.W. All very calm and peaceful until about six this morning when it started to pour with rain. The glass has been dropping like a stone at about $1\frac{1}{2}$ points an hour, 18 in the last day and the wind has now headed us and we are wallowing around with the jib and well-reefed mainsail. Last night there was an incredible sunset with the afterglow holding on till three in the morning B.S.T. Under an hour later the sun was on its first raising legs, fighting for the surface. Half a dozen dolphins were with us just after lunch.

My patch on the leak by the starboard chainplates seems to be reasonably successful in that we were not pumping quite so much this morning. Whenever the sea comes up to the starboard rail, water just pours in. 100 strokes an hour on the whale pump — hard work but it certainly shifts water — a bathful every two minutes. We must be taking 200 gallons an hour at times (worst) six-and-a-half a minute — one gallon every ten seconds — a pint a second, quite a thought. Imagine having half a dozen of you each with milk bottles throwing in a pint every six seconds, quite a nightmare.

It looks as if we will be hove to again for twelve hours. It seems to be a monotonous pattern about these days, becalmed, moderately good wind, hove to. . . . The glass looks as if it is levelling out, and will level out to 997. The depression is going north of us. Let's hope the next goes to the south to speed us on our way — mind you, we have been lucky to have them pass near us at all giving south-westerly winds (gale force winds). We sit and read, talking little. The library is very nearly bare now, and the Old Man is reading *The Magus*, having had *Clayhanger*, *First Circle*, *Most Secret*, and most of the others already. I hate to imagine what he thinks of it — cock and bull no doubt. I should now be up to 10,000 words, cock also, my first novel or How Baroque got to Greenland — if we ever get there. Looking at the Atlantic chart it looks as if we still have oodles of thousands of miles to do. Cape Farewell will not be seen, as the Pilot advises all and sundry to keep miles and miles away from it, for what reason I'm not sure and cannot be bothered to get up and look. Icebergs apparently — what they do there I don't know — down the west coast and up the east.

Thursday, 5th July — Very cold last night. I had shorts, jersey, shirt and oilskins on and was O.K. except for the hands. These large boots of mine make all the difference to the warmth of the feet, with no point of the rubber touching the sock, and one of those false soles. Have my red towelling socks on, very effective when clean, what they will be like in a week's time I don't like to think. No washing of any sort goes on on board, the skipper shaves occasionally but no one else. One's hands get a little cleaner on washing up, but that's about all. I have a pair of socks draped over the doghouse that I hope will be washed first in salt water, then in rain, then sun-dried and aired — all very romantic but I think the process is going to take many months. Have just had a sharp reprimand. 'On watch means On watch, not writing novels' as I was in the nice warm doghouse. All very seamanlike, but one becomes lazy in the ocean miles from anywhere with the tiller lashed and the boat gently ploughing to leeward, (Lourdes). It's N.N.W. 5 at the moment, and we are making nearly three points of leeway at times. I think we would be better hove to, and then we could all have a really good night's sleep — never! — I think this is what makes the Old Man go on and on — rigorous self-discipline. We are now coming up to ten days at sea, almost the longest period I have ever spent, but this is somewhat different from motor-sailing down to Gibraltar.

Have just taken my first real live sextant sight. Not the best day to start on but the figure I produced received the comment, 'That's about right' from the skipper, fair enough I reckon from the expert for a first attempt. All very easy, except that Brian's machine is so heavy; but the rolling boat does not seem to make a lot of difference, it's just the fact of holding the thing up to your face while you find (a) the horizon and (b) the sea. I think I shall pursue the practice further, and then start worrying about how you work it out, and, more ridiculous, the theory; whereas before I knew a fair amount of the theory, almost nothing of practice, and absolutely nothing of actually measuring the angle.

Ilan has suggested that I fling in a few short stories to pad out the hard facts. I probably will at some stage, but the conditions we live in, although producing flights of fancy, seem to be taking me back to places I've been to and people, all past events, hardly fantasy, the real miraging has not yet started. I don't yet yearn for anything I haven't got, probably because I have convinced myself that this curious life is somewhere near perfection when a little of the glamour and romance has been stuffed back into the cold unyielding elemental atmosphere that abounds.

Hove to at sea at six o'clock yet again. We are pumping vast quantities of water in the starboard tack, all coming in up high near the rubbing strake. I reckon we must take the whole lot off at Godthaab and caulk it all. We should be in for a reasonably comfortable night even if we are making seven points of leeway. I find the skipper's moonsight was only three minutes different from mine — I did it a minute or two after as well.

Friday, 6th July — At four a.m. it is light enough to see one's way round the boat, but to write in the deckhouse I have the paraffin light going. The door is shut to keep the freezing cold draught out. The glass has been twenty points from 999 in the last 36 hours, but the weather has not improved at all, and we lose in leeway to the south with just a little westing made, but precious little. We read Brown's

Nautical Almanac gleaning knowledge for 'Advice of Officers on the instruction of mixing paints', designed for the mid-nineteenth century. She rides over all these waves with amazing ease — I hope it will be the same for the big seas that we will probably run into on the way back. The skipper was telling me how it took him a week to get from the Scillies to Lymington because of the light headwinds — very infuriating after so long at sea — one imagines one is home once in the Channel, although it is probably one of the most hazardous parts of the voyage, with supertankers and lack of sea room.

We are moving again at last. S.S.W. and two points of variation on our side, so that is not far off our rhumb line. It is going to be one of the dark days, no sun, no warmth. We will no doubt be becalmed by 4.30 p.m. just in time for afternoon tea, eaten off the floor, mind you, but still always at 4.30. The skipper is singing again. You can always tell when he's on watch, his deep croaky voice and his stamping foot — never together — it's an excellent method of keeping the feet warm and passing the time, about 1,200 to the hour. Wind backed, gone about, wind picked up making N.N.W., barometer high, should start dropping again soon. There are two people on board, mainly the Skipper, who pull in the jib at every opportunity so as to make the staysail almost redundant. As I almost always steer from the leeward side I can almost always see the staysail. I also keep warmer as I am protected by the doghouse to some extent. We have been averaging fifty miles a day so far and are almost there. Half way to Cape Farewell anyway — well, almost half way to Cape Farewell. Farvel, Marvel, revolting stuff. We have some other curious stuff which is really good in custard, once a month; reasonable in porridge every other day, and revolting in tea and coffee. Tea is black as pitch — speaking of which, have just found another hole in the sheer strake, where two planks meet. I expect when we take off the rubbing strake we will find hundreds of other holes, as it fairly pours in on both tacks — no doubt in about a year's time the Old Man will have found them all, and it will be safe to heel her right over and thrash to windward, for which purpose she was designed back in '02.

I am certain I should try and put down the fantasies I have about my boat. I feel I have so much worked out in hard fact of where things should go, down to the last saucepan and oil line. I feel that I could write a book about it, but I just cannot start anywhere — perhaps I should start on another fantasy, and try and capture it from the start, and try and trace it through on paper as I cannot do in my mind, as I have not the self-discipline that Ilan seems to have. We talk a lot about simple subconscious ideas, and I become totally confused as words do not seem to be able to explain ideas of one's own as one would like to put them across — like the light-switch in Brodhurst's study, one stared at it to counter-weigh the advice that was being flung at one, while one's subconscious was miles away — rather like looking into a flare, or at the sea — sounds on a beach — looking through it — trance-like.

Saturday, 7th July — Started reducing sail at 0200 hours. Now down to jib 03 reef main, fair wind abaft the beam, incredible. Heave to soon, I suppose. The glass drops like a stone, southerly wind, warm wind from the tropics. Next year to the Antarctic through the tropics. 83 days to Montevideo — perhaps. I suppose I might be anywhere this time next year — in London back at University — flying to the moon. . . . The wind dropped at midday. Have just taken my first meridian and worked it out, all very easy. Take angle, add or subtract sextant error look up tables for correcting altitude of some lower limb for height of eye above sea level, add that, subtract total from 90 degrees add declination, and whizbang out comes latitude. It couldn't be easier, all I need to do now is to find out about longitude and I'm away. The most difficult thing at the moment is to find the sea and horizon at the same time, especially when it is overcast as it is at the moment and so often is in the North Atlantic.

Fantasy Boat

Layout and function of engine room controls. Main engine 150 H.P. Generator 50 H.P. Capable of running 15 K.A.V. generator on air compressor also to have main reduction drive to start main engine which is compressed air start. Also for air compressor to recharge bottles should necessity arise, and engine also to run lathe direct. Main fueltank just forward of engine room bulkhead, and also in engine room to feed galley, directly above, wheelhouse also directly above to facilitate easy controls, battery bank also in engine room.

Sunday 8th July — We are in thick fog since the non-existent dawn. The stove went on today to see if we can dry out the place a little. It has no effect unless one comes in from the outside when there is a glimmer of warmth. Oh for a Tilley lamp or two. I think the Skipper must be getting soft. Brian tells me that last year one felt as if one was trespassing on his ground just by being on board. Last night he put her right aback, and the log line got wrapped around something far under water, and we had to break the rope. It took two of us an hour and a half to get it back in the water. Entry for the log: put her aback, log line caught, tut tut. He even apologised for doing it. It all seemed very unlikely to me, I think the rot really must have set in.

Monday, 9th July — Sister's birthday — thinking about her wedding, hoping all will go well. It looks as if there is a possibility of getting home if we get to Godthaab on the 26th July. Romantic thoughts of arriving London Airport at 9.00 in the morning, taking a taxi home and staying Saturday night (who with?) and flying back to Greenland on Sunday — quite a contrast. The thick fog persists, and we have a fair wind (gentle) to push us in the right direction. It has lasted for 24 hours already and I hope it won't go on for a week. The Skipper was in fog for a week last year just south of Iceland. This caused the great '71 mutiny, that everyone knows of. I am certain he made a mess of his meridian sight yesterday by forgetting to add on anything for height of eye. I got the same altitude as he, but a totally different latitude, and it looks in his calculations as if he has forgotten to add in that extra 15 minutes. In fog one should be as near sea level as possible, so as to see the actual horizon, whereas in sun one should be as high as possible to see the actual horizon, i.e. on top of a wave. Brian and I read Mary Blewitt furiously to learn all the technical data in order to understand what is happening (regularly). It is cold now with the air temperature down to about 9° and sea at 10°, hence the fog. If cold now, what will it be like in a month's time? I hate to think. I actually shivered very briefly on watch early this morning. The warmest position I have found outside my bedroll is sitting on my famous homemade seat in the corner of the cockpit with my feet up on the deck. If one stands up one's feet get cold. I have not covered over my jersey inside my oilskins and don't suffer much. It will be very pleasant to get some mail and hear how all is back home. Also quite nice to have a full night's sleep.

Have just spent all the afternoon trying to fathom out the Marine sight reduction tables, and have, I think, succeeded in that I can now find my position, time, and distance. Time calculate G.H.A. — calculate L.H.A. = G.H.A. + A.S.S. Long.E. where L.H.A. is whole number, so got A.S.S. Long.E. Assume integral latitude. Feed in L.H.A. A.S.S. Lat. and declination into tables and out will come H.C.

d and Z. Rule about Z. on every page to work out Zn:d is Altitude difference so feed into interpolation table H.C. (for whole number of degrees) to find out actual Hc (Tabulated Altitude) (If Lat. same as dec., then Lat. and dec. both north and south). True altitude (corrected sextant reading) Hc = distance towards sun from assumed position (if sun is tve) Zn = angle of position line.

Angle and distance of position line is taken from assumed position not D.R. Clink, clink, clunk. All very easy when you know how and have a boat, sextant, sight reduction tables, Almanac, sun, open sea etc. Thinking of a sextant, I don't see why one shouldn't make one correct to the nearest half minute — anything that moves and has a vernier scale on it from a chemistry or physics laboratory. Have just worked out complete intercept sight with assumed reasonable accuracy.

Tuesday, 10th July — The fog is still with us and we make very good progress averaging $3\frac{1}{2}$ knots in the right direction. It is almost incredible. The fog cleared a little this afternoon and the wind backed southerly and we are disappearing in a cloud of spray in the right direction. We have lost the cycles of wind – hove to – calm that pursued us for the first week out and we have now had fair wind for three days and have done about 250 miles. This puts us in a position about 350 miles E.S.E. of Kap Farvel. It will be terrible if we have to go about to get south of the Cape but there is little we can do about it. A northerly wind now would just about do the trick — we have hardly been on the port tack since leaving, and it makes getting into my roll a bit of a problem owing to the limited headroom. Things get better, down wind and having to drop staysail and put three rolls in.

Wednesday, 11th July — The mist, fog, haze is still with us and is beginning to get a bit tedious really. We are now fifty miles too far north of where we ought to be with the wind in the south west, which isn't very helpful to us. Have not had a meridian for three days, but might be lucky today. All aboard is damp and cold from this wet fog, but I suppose it can't go on forever — can't it? The chafe is over-setting us, lots of rope wearing through getting old. The jib halyard must be replaced. Brave little me will have to go aloft when it is much calmer to get the block down. It must then be put up again — no I won't spend half an hour up there waiting while someone puts an eyesplice in the polyprop rope. We have averaged 81 miles a day while the fog has been here — our best three days and we averaged only 3½ knots.

Thursday, 12th July — We hove to last night at 7.00, as the glass went up so did the wind. It reached gale force during the night and is now down to Force 6/7. Always we have had the blows on rapidly rising glasses. This time it is from the west and producing some pretty large seas but no bigger than the ones in the channel — nothing to write home about — we carry six rolls in the main and the staysail as per usual, but the staysail is much too large and we lay almost a-hull if there are a few large blasts in a row. It is amazing how dry these boats are — I remember Colin Putt telling me this when we were in Mylor, I didn't believe a word of it. All foredecks are wet as far as I am concerned, why should this be an exception. However, I did get a bootful last night and emptied about ½ pint of water out of my right boot. I wrapped the offending sock up in a small towel and stuffed it into my pants, and within four hours it was dry enough to wear and not feel the icy cold of wet water. My trousers are totally damp with the flares being almost wet at times.

17 22 57 = G.M.T.	Alt.	4250	D.R.			36 21 W
		12	dec.			
73 36 5		———				
		4302				
+ 5 44 3		———				
———						
79 21 = G.H.A.						
− 36 21	Hc		d	Z	Zn = 239	
———	41	44.3	+ 53.4	121		
43 = L.H.A.		45.8	4302			
———		1.8	4232			
		———	———			
		92.32.0	30 towards			

This is approximately right. The sight was taken in a Force 7 so things are improving. The fog has certainly cleared and I am now getting the hang of working out the sights. The great difficulty now is getting an accurate enough fix to rely on, the calculation is easy and the little appendages will follow in time, stars, moon, variation, meridian passages, great circles, plotting charts, the lot, all easy when you know how, as the actress said to the Bishop.

Friday 13th. Friday 13th. Started sailing after breakfast as per usual. In 36 hours we lost about 70 miles to the south, take the rough with the smooth I suppose. We are only making south-west at the moment in a vast swell. Jonno sings, sings and drives us mad. We were wondering about the Skipper's pet fear, the mainsheet parting. I reckon that you drop the bloody thing as quickly as possible before it goes through the gallows and doghouse. If it started swinging somewhere near the boat nothing would stop it. It would be virtually impossible to capture the bugger and get control of it. On all points of sailing it would blow out to leeward and not over the boat. Going down wind would cause a bit of havoc on the shrouds — tricky problem. Becalmed by midnight, it looks like the usual routine. Becalmed, favourable wind, hove to.

Saturday, 14th July — Bastille day for what it is worth. We motored 10 miles this morning which has brought us a most favourable wind 7 knots (of winds, that is) from south of east. About 9.30 last night I saw my first ever whale. He (she) was about 25 feet long. Rather like love and arterial bleeding, you know that it is a whale, pitch black and the whole of his back out of the water when surfacing, most dramatic, he came up about three times about 15–20 feet away. A great surge of water, exhaling of air and all the time a gentle rhythmic pattern that all whales all over the world must possess. All very dramatic, a little frightening (awe inspiring). The damage that a powerful animal like that could do is immense. Even the biggest porpoises we saw, about 15 feet long, could accidentally put a hole in the bottom of the boat with no bother at all. I saw one of these very large ones disappear under the boat from about 6 feet away and ideas of Bill King and the Robertson people came to mind. The Old Man had a large whale follow him for two days in the Indian Ocean staying dead astern from about 20 feet away. It must be terrible to hear this vast beast at night, not being able to see him, only the turbulence in the water and a rush of air. The noise of the gust of air from the one I saw first brought my attention to it. This very loud noise, I look round and see the whole sea displaced and a black, shiny moving back, taking its place.

We were comparing Cape Farewell to the Horn and the difficulties of rounding it just after the westerly blow (gale). When asked, 'Have you been round the Horn (which Horn)?' 'No, I've been south of it.'

500 miles south. Quite a natural occurrence for the Old Man. He firmly says that there are almost no gales there in summer and that it was calm when he saw it last.

dec 22 40 say 90 $(x + 9) + 2240 = x$

90 + 2231 = 2x = 11231 so that when at 66 15 north approximately meridian time altitude should equal $x = 66$ 15 N. Latitude, very interesting Saturday. Becalmed all today and spent the morning repairing all odds and ends, a splice in the jib halyard, replacing mainsheet, still about 30 feet too short, but better than nothing. The porpoises started jumping last night so perhaps we are in for some wind. I picked up a slow morse signal on 389 Kz 02 N. Can't work out what it is. Greenland definitely but so loud 200 miles away at least. We can place it as we go round Cape Farewell and use it on the way back, likely story, just about as probable as Jonah and the whale. We are now into a new chart (great improvement) which has Greenland, Labrador, Newfoundland etc. and the Atlantic is now behind us. Well, almost.

Sunday, 15th July — The glass is still high and we are still becalmed (half knot) 36 hours in a glassy foggy sea in the northern latitudes of the North Atlantic — ridiculous — it should start blowing soon from the south-west if my predictions are correct. Brian woke me, as always, at six this morning. We were heading south-east all aback with the faintest breeze (0) from the south-west. It took me an hour and a quarter to turn the boat round, to start with. I tried gybing her and then tacking her. Observing the ship to be travelling backwards I again tried gybing her, putting the tiller over the other way where it was held by back-pressure till we started moving forward — no success there, would you believe it, tacking her. This surprisingly worked, all done from the cockpit. I had to hold the staysail aback till 7 points off the wind or she just swung back. She seems to like going backwards, which usually means that when something of this ilk happens one turns the tiller the wrong way. I was contemplating getting one of the oars out, it would have been much quicker in the long run, we must try them one day.

Ulysses is almost ended unfortunately, I was really beginning to enjoy the glommeration of words, but I am now on the last lap, and the *Clayhanger* is in sight. It is a book I shall read again before the trip is out as I gleaned so little from it this time. It is rather like the Bible, pick it up, open it indiscriminately and read ten pages, 100 pages, enjoy yourself, sleep, wake up. . . .

The fog descended at midday. The wind has come, perhaps we will have three days of this to get us past Farewell, who knows. Have been studying the moon-sight procedure. Just a few more increments and corrections and interpolations to compute. The stars seem easier, all fixed around Aries. . . . Just look it up somewhere. If declination star is less than $3°$ then one's in business. The sea has a give and take relation with sailors it seems, you take what's given and give what's taken. (The Old Man takes but does not give — the Old Man and the Sea, perhaps.) This entails seizing every opportunity to take, and fighting against giving. Terrible idea really, but that's what it amounts to. For strong wind you must force every mile out of her, and with strong adverse winds fight to stop losing too much ground. We lost a reasonable day's run in that gale. This morning I fought to get half a knot out of her — a relentless challenge, numinous (awe?). At 15.30 I returned triumphant to Ithaca.

Monday, 16th July — We now tool along at 4 knots gently on course in fog and rain as per usual. Discussion on distance of Kap Farvel from England, Great Circle route Seven stones 50.04 N. 6.04 W. to Kap Farvel 59.46 43.54 Enter 50 as latitude argument $37°50$ (difference longitude) as L.M.A. argument $(38°)$ and 5946 as declination Hc = 66 33 9 dc — 7.2 Z = 52.9.

(90 − 6) = 24 24 × 60 = distance = 1440 miles. Initial direction 360 − 53 = $307°$. There are about four totally separate cases to be known, it's not a lot of help as we can't sail on G.C.R. We should know where we are, and we know where Cape Farewell is and as we aren't going within sight of Cape Farewell (60 miles) it does not really help at all. The problem of the half apparent mountain looming over the horizon is past.

Tuesday, 17th July — Foggy, southerly winds. Good day's run yesterday, average 3 knots all day, incredible, wind now S.S.E., dead astern, slowly. We have definitely made Kap Farvel about 90 miles to the north. We turn northwards a little but not much owing to enormous variation, nearly forty degrees. We have been on an even keel now for about 3 days, but making as much progress as ever. Saw a glimpse of the moon last night through the mist and drizzle and gloom. We have hardly seen the sun for more than 5 minutes for what seems like weeks. It now gets dark little, although sunrise is at about 7.00 a.m. G.M.T. and sunset about 1.30 a.m. owing to our curious time, but we have not seen the sun on the horizon for ten days at least, not felt the heat of his rays.

I find in my timetables that if I leave Sondre Stromfjord on Friday at midday I can be in London at 3.00 a.m. on Saturday morning, and if I leave London at midnight on Sunday, I can be in Sondre Stromfjord midday Monday, O.K. assuming that one can get from Godthaab to Sondre Stromfjord easily if at all. If by chance we arrive on Thursday I should be able to do it. All very romantic — walking cheerfully over the face of the world and all that. We have almost officially turned north to Godthaab — hardly north. We hear over the radio that there are reports of waterspouts 200 feet high in the channel, while we have almost favourable wind heading N.N.W. Magnetic N.W.X.W. T. one. Close hauled port tack as per usual wind Force 3 increasing. Let's hope it does not blow up and land us east of Cape Farewell again. It's still foggy. It cleared this morning but still this great swell. It must have something to do with the waterspouts — a great depression sweeping in from the Atlantic, hurricane force winds and us moving gently, mostly becalmed with the glass falling, falling.

Have had *Clayhanger* as a change from *Ulysses* and finished it in two days. I suppose I must read the other two parts of the Trilogy to finish the job off. When I don't know, never perhaps. All very romantic but too finicky for my liking. Not enough rhythm although one can read it in just a few days and enjoy it. Edwin's character and Father's is put over very well, but it is too calculated. The bit in the introduction (read after) shows how mathematically the book was set out and carefully written — a week allowed for chapter, 1000 words a day, that sort of thing.

I wait for the ice. Yesterday saw a few large chunks of timber and many birds in flocks like seagulls, about 2 dozen. The D.F. signs are clear, very clear, so we know we are almost there, although we still have another 300 or so miles to do to Godthaab. John talks of his rump steak and hamburgers, totally discontented with life, no, not life, just the food and other people's stupidity, ours. He shoots his ball that much. A custard pie, not set, is in the offing. It has been hanging up outside and now inside rattling and swinging rapidly and precarious in all directions, no doubt it will be very good. We must find a way to stop the oven burning things.

Wednesday, 18th July — Last night we hove to in the fog as the wind was heading us too much for us to keep south of the admiralty limit. At 02.00 in the morning the fog cleared and on we go. The sun is almost out and Jonno actually saw a sunrise; first time for weeks. If visibility were very good we would be bound to see lee or land. Wind is getting up now (p.m.) and heading us, which isn't too helpful. The Old Man sleeps totally encompassed by his sleeping bag in a foetal position, occasionally his head sticks out and he looks even more foetal — large head on small body, hand near mouth as if sucking thumb. Yesterday I told him about this wedding business and how it is beginning to look remotely possible, and he got the wrong end of the stick completely, 'You want to leave the voyage do you?' 'No, no!' I cried. In the end he seemed to appreciate that I did not really want to go (cost, delay, bother etc.) but my conscience told me that I must if possible. The more I think about it though the more I would like to be there when my sister goes — how much pleasure it would give Mother and perhaps Selina and all friends and relations. The others think it a good idea so that they will have a chance of seeing Godthaab properly and not just there to pick up mail, food, and plug a few of the leaks. At nine this evening we are 40 miles from the coast, although we can see nothing of it yet. One can in theory — there are 5,000 foot mountains with a range of 70, perhaps 80, miles.

Great debates about the French bomb — should they be allowed to turn people out of water that does not belong to them? I think that it is a good thing.

Thursday, 19th July — The great day has arrived — ice was seen at about 12.30 this afternoon — a little triangular shaped piece stuck out on the horizon, partially engloomed by the torrential rain that has been pouring down most of the night owing to sea breezes. Land was vaguely seen this evening but all overcast as usual. There is now another large one looking like a large aeroplane, bright against a typical non-horizon. Very exciting really — what we have come here for. None of this clear outlined stuff, blurred light yet green coloured, probably 3 miles off, mind you, ineluctable. We have been spoilt these last 10 days, no heaving around in the middle of the night with wet clothes and wet sleeping bags. We are here anyway — part of the object has been achieved — we can turn round and go back again now except we are running out of twice baked bread. At four o'clock there was an extremely violent squall, just as we were about to reef. It was possible to feel the wind increasing with Ilan struggling with the helm.

We unknowingly passed a chunk of ice during this operation while heaving to. Now at six o'clock there are large floes all round us, half a mile long and a few hundred feet high, all incredibly beautiful, the angular bergs (one almost perfectly pyramid) looking like the north face of the Eiger, and the large floes looking like a ridge in the Lakes all covered with snow, windswept. Some are greeny-white, some bluey-white. The outline of the land is just visible; when the visibility was not so good they merged into the horizon. It was incredible when the mist and gloom cleared and all the sharp outlines made the sea even starker. They certainly give one something to look at during one's watch, also to measure one's progress. The sea temperature at noon was 6.75 at six o'clock it is o.5. We are now obviously in the east-west Greenland current, the air is under 40°F but dry and very bearable. An incredible change though, one minute we might be in the Channel and next we have ice on all sides. There are, I suppose, 8 large floes in sight and no doubt many very small pieces. It reminds me of the Yugoslav coast, hundreds of small islands apparently scattered randomly in the sea with the coast behind, just in the distance. At ten o'clock the fog descended, all in bursts. Brian appears and says that we had better go about and goes up on deck again. Half a minute later a shout — 'you'd better hurry!' The Skipper and I both heaved ourselves rapidly out of beds and then wasted another ten seconds getting our boots on — must die with your boots on — 75 yards away was an iceberg about 200 yards long and 40 yards wide, luckily no vast tongues were sticking out to bar our way. We did not have to jybe — just — we hove to after this and will probably do so if fog descends. It's the bane of our lives, it's either overcast or foggy. When the skies do clear though the scenery will be fantastic, stark and real.

Having been, Friday 20th July, in ice for a day one feels as if one has been here for months. Last night was the coldest so far, sea down to 0.25 C and air down about 1.75 — all really cold — one's feet are worst hit. Hands seem to bear up O.K. Perhaps a clean pair of socks might do the trick, or just don't bother. The watches pass very quickly. Perhaps the cold clears the mind — like the firing squad — so one can think clearly and just let one's thoughts run on, also one concentrates much harder on what one is about to run into and how cold one's feet aren't. We don't know exactly where we are — about 30 miles off the bit of coast that runs east-west of Cape Farewell. At ten o'clock this evening we have brought the grand day's total up to 10 miles, 6 of which were done by the industrious use of the engine. The sails flap, the gentle swell shifts the boat and the gaff screams back and forth shaking the boom and gooseneck. We have had the fire on all day today although it has not been really cold (not really been cold), about 5° on the celsius scale. Ilan produced a lasagne this evening that was really very good and hot and a lot of it. He manages really well on little variation — sardines, pilchards, cheese, peanut butter, marmite for lunch, dried cabbage, carrots, potatoes, onions, corned beef, spam, sausages in brine and a few other sundries. This is not his only attraction. He's always happy, content, satisfied and cheerful.

Saturday, 21st July — Well, we might get to Godthaab at this rate but how we will get back against the current I don't know. We travelled at about three quarters of a knot for the last 12 hours. Nine miles — home to Winchester! — and we have the distance from London to Manchester to do. There is no ice, no fog, no sun, only rain, whales and plankton. Curious looking plankton it is, too, large amoebid-looking things. At night each particular one shows up by its phosphorescence and glows much longer than your ordinary plank-tons. I must do some more fishing to see if I can catch a salmon or cod or whale or something. There is a lot of fishing to be done on our way up Davis Strait, about four large banks just near the coast where the Germans, Poles and Norwegians come in their large trawlers, the Faeroese come in off boats and handline and the Portuguese are supposed to come here in large schooners. I hope we will see one if there are any. They can't manage very well under sail alone, I shouldn't think. We have done the whole of ten miles since midnight last night, so in the last 48 hours twenty miles and a bit of current, and only two bags of bread left Oh dear! One of my predictions is manifesting itself — the swivel on the end of the boom is pulling off along with the tiller getting worse and worse every day. I'm not sure if I dare pull it off and see what the matter is in case it does not go back — horror of horrors — we will have to do something about the boom fitting, though, because if that goes we will be in trouble — the Skipper's great fear come true. It certainly won't help if it does work loose.

    A wind has just come, if you could call it that, a knot I suppose, all helps at these sort of speeds. We have about 200 miles to go to Godthaab according to the Old Man's sight at 3.00 p.m. — almost the meridian which helped — the only sun of the day. It has been warm all day. The fog has come down very thick about 50 yards off and a berg bit appeared about 30 yards away. We are only moving at about half a knot and the engine is all ready to run . . . just hit the bottom and put her in gear — sounds easy — all ready for action.

Sunday 22nd July — Yesterday's sights put us somewhere on the central plateau and we were a bit nervous all last night. Head wind has sprung up since midnight but we held our course due north all night. At eleven this morning there were many bergs and suddenly one of the largest ones was an island. We gybed quickly as visibility was only about half a mile, as much as it's ever been. The sun immediately came out and the Skipper took a sight which put us at one of about half-a-dozen islands about 20 miles south of Frederikshaab, so we have had a good push along by the current. If only the wind would change to about the south-east we would be in business. The twice baked bread is about to run out, and Ilan has put his hand to baking some, which we will try for tea. A cold wind blows and burns the ears when out of it — just like a frosty winter's morning — not really unpleasant but good to get out of — a very dry cold that makes life bearable. It is such a pity that the fog is here or we would be able to see the land and shore and where we are. Have passed quite a few bergs this morning, some very smooth, some jagged at the edges, but all with beautiful curves. Maare has nothing on these. The colour of the water just near them where the tongues stick out is light green, very very clear. When we throw tins over you can watch them go down and down through the seemingly black water (just deep).

The bread was very good, hard on the outside, doughy on the inside. Made of baking powder and not yeast, so one cannot expect much, very edible and commendable, we could march a long way on it.

I have religiously been keeping a barometric chart and have come to the conclusion that when the glass drops the wind veers in this part of the world in mid July 1972.

Monday, 23rd July — Back in the ice again having tacked all yesterday afternoon, due west. The air was clear all morning and we could see the mountain tops 0 (?6)°15 North about 18 miles off. 16 bergs in view at one stage, very distinctly outlined but not with the sun on them. I suppose one day we will see them in all their glory, bright sun, pack-ice in distance, mountains with snow, eskimos in kyacks etc. The fog we are getting used to, it is not as dismal as I would have thought. It doesn't get on one's nerves all the time it's just there. It's nearly two weeks now that we have had it almost continually. Gazing at an old Star Chart of about 1930 I find to my amazement, as in the Prayer Book, Golden Number = TEM 1973 + 1/19 = 7*

Epact = V($17^* \times 11$) −X30 = 8 TEM 187/30 = 7

To 7 add 23 as day of month + 7 for July − X30 = 7 for moon's age moon's age × 48/60 = time of meridian = 336/60 = 5 hours 36 minutes

The 5 hours 36 minutes is correct or nearly 5 hours 46 minutes to be exact, but the 7 is wrong. Oh well, that's the rule. It has much other information which is just as well left on the chart as copied, as one would not be able to learn it just by writing it down. All about barometric means, not to speak of all about the stars. One day, I suppose, I shall start when the skies get clearer and there is not much else to do. Browns has a simple bit on star identification, perhaps I'll start on that.

Tuesday, 23rd July — 90 miles to go due north. A lovely sunny morning, no wind, totally becalmed. The floor was cleaned, I shaved and brushed my teeth. The Old Man grumpy again. Everything cheerful and not quite so cold. As cold as Pen Piercy's house usually is when there is no fire. I think I found how to combat the cold feet problem at night, standing only on one's heels with no other part of the foot touching the boot. Only one problem, you can't see where you are going, which is O.K. in mid-Atlantic, but not so good in ice.

What little wind there is now is making the shrouds hum loudly as if a submarine is directly underneath. There is a tabular berg ahead which we might reach this afternoon. Just shape tabular, like a table, mensa mensam etc.

Am now about halfway through *1st Circle* which must be good for me. I find myself reading it at odd hours of the day and night and enjoying it, not the bits about the cold in Siberia though, as it makes it slightly more real almost being in Arctic wastes. So far (6.00 p.m.) we have made 40 miles (not in the right direction), thick fog since about 10.00 o'clock. I realise now how great my watch was this morning, just like a summer's morning in England, clear very early. The air is so clear up here it is unbelievable. The Skipper had to use almost all the shades in his sextant when taking a sight at 8.00 p.m. He has been writing almost continuously all today and yesterday. It seems to be his best way of self-expression. I feel just like a schoolboy. He glowers around the place and one imagines him writing on us all. There was a fog bow this morning for about an hour directly down sun of us, smaller diameter than a rainbow and very bright, totally white semicircle — seriously impressive — it is only small things like this along with the food Ilan produces that keep boredom at bay. It is too cold to work successfully on deck although much needs doing — checking, cleaning, painting, scraping caulking etc. We have averaged 59 miles a day since leaving Ireland. Pretty appalling really, but then it is about as fast as walking, 2–3 knots.

Wednesday 24th July — A fair wind this morning by 4 o'clock. At 10.00 a.m. we are steaming down wind at 6 knots at which another squall hit us, passed stations, hove to to reef with the bloody boom-end fitting jamming yet again, and let her go again; at which the Skipper goes down, has a look at the charts, and appears saying there should be land in sight. Land is in sight. Passing stations, jybe we round, as always keeping the weather topping-lift on, which frightens me — I imagine the gaff parting — not a pleasant idea, but it's that or letting it swing right across and pulling the top mast off, most unpleasant. We decide, in the warmth of the saloon, that we should have stood on and made sure of an identification. This Davis Strait is just like the Mediterranean without the fog, flat calm for days and then sudden fall in barometer which no one notices and a hopeless squall appears behind one's back and then subsides back to Force 4. Four o'clock and on we run. Fifty miles to go, ten hours if this holds. Dawn tomorrow we might see the lights. The Old Man has started writing letters furiously — we must obviously be near land. I have been playing around with the D.F. set but all the stations are in straight lines with us so that does not help to get a cross bearing. I am trying in vain to remember the rule of thumb for the angle of one's fingers held at arm's length. I shall have to write it out I suppose — tangent angles will no doubt help.

thumb 4 lines 1st finger 3 tons 2nd 3 tons 3rd 3 tons little 3 tons total wide width 16 tons common to all take 24 tons

Thursday, 26th July — Hove to all last night but becalmed at midnight having made a landfall 20 miles south of Godthaab. The fog came down at six and after breakfast we started sailing north, then motoring, the fog started to clear and at midday we saw a few islands and headed east, to find ourselves among about a hundred small islands all unidentifiable. Took a sight and turned back south and picked up a few of the leading marks, lighthouses about 30 feet, a prominent radio mast, now two of them which does not help, hundreds of other beacons, masts, islands, all unidentifiable except one on the outermost island for which we head to save neuroticism. It is now about 15 miles up the fjord to Godthaab itself—it now being 2.15 p.m. so we should be there at say, 5.30 p.m. or 4.30 p.m. their time. The gods have obviously had their way in deciding about the wedding. All they must supply now is a helicopter to Stromfjord, and a seat on the plane to Copenhagen and London. This will mean that I should be back Monday p.m. which should be O.K. by the Old Man. I haven't mentioned it to him since the first time, but I reckon he's remembered. We are now 3.30 pm. well into the fjord, and the end is in sight — not really end but a beginning. By August 1st we will be on our way really north, getting out of the fog and into the wilds of Disko — a month late — half the time scheduled for the trip up the coast will be gone. Sad really, one ought to be spending the whole summer up here not having to worry about small things like winter gales in the Atlantic. The Old Man has been up on deck since about 10.00 a.m. looking, reading, searching, happy even (perhaps). I suppose he can't really be content with it all, motoring for so many hours, upset by us all. 'Anchovies 520' up against a wall.

The city, town, village is a mile away apparently. There is a fish factory where we are, quite a few large boats up to 200 tons and numerous fishing boats, rows of green painted flats in low blocks and that's all. The Old Man immediately sent to find the Harbour Master who appeared plus assistant in suit and fast small motorboat. The terrain is simply barren — patches of snow and the rest is just bare rock. It must be really dismal in winter, no light, snow, ice, cloud and nothing else, still very beautiful in its solitude. 'Mischief' is written up on the cliff face, which made the Skipper sad. 'I almost wept when I saw it.' Not surprising, he talks of her as a lost friend which she was, a home for 15 years or so. He does not want to come out tonight but tells us to piss off, where to I can't imagine. Go into town, I suppose, about a mile away. I shall go and have a look to see where the airport is, and post office, and if possible find out the time(s) of helicopters to Stromfjord.

I feel really whacked. It's been a long day anyway and I was up all last night, but one always feels tired when arriving at a port, new movements, rushing around, a lot of thought about what has to be done and doing it. I should get more than six hours sleep tonight, we have just put the clocks back another hour so it is 9.00 p.m. in England. Perhaps I might be able to ring up England tonight and see how things stand.

Friday 27th July — Up at 5.30 a.m. to go to airport, if you can call it that, to see if by chance there was any change on last night's pronouncement of no seats, no chance. All very friendly. It is a very modern Heliport, rather like a new up-to-date South American one, just a waiting room, loo, pair of oversize bathroom scales and a small office. The helicopter can carry 16 passengers and I watched each one, talked to a few, as they prepared to walk out onto the take-off pad. I am beginning to like very much all that I see here, the people are cheerful and happy, speak English (all Danes). I sent off three telegrams today which set me back somewhat, 50 words in one of them, also some champagne and caviar to have at noon tomorrow, or 3.00 o'clock wedding time, I presume it will be at those anyway. Was disappointed by the mail I didn't receive, only 2 letters — not loved like I used to be — good old Jane, loving to the end, just like Mama. The telegram should keep people reasonably happy — cost enough. I hope it all goes well anyway. People all coming from far and near to send off the happy pair. I hope they are happy. I must start on the letter-writing soon. I don't feel like doing it now but no doubt I will get into the swing once started. Decide on letters to whom, postcards to others first or both. . . . Curious how I can go on writing this journal but not want to inform people of the journey, my happiness etc. I was hoping to be able to do it on the plane.

Saturday, 28th July — Well this is to be the great day and I am not there to share it. I did my best but there is nothing else I can do. We look round Godthaab buying books, postcards, putty and diesel oil. The whole town is just like a South American one, completely unco-ordinated, low buildings scattered regardlessly on the rock. More modern than South America but the same sort of atmosphere — cut off — no roads leading out, only the airport and harbour. The buildings are built of concrete and wood — there is only one stone house around, which is five hundred years old. Everything comes from Denmark, France or England. There seem to be no exports or even self-sufficiencies produced near here, few fresh vegetables, even some water comes by sea. It's as if it is a garden city, fed from an independent source. The food stores are Danish-looking, neat clean smart — only when one gets to places where nails and things are sold does one find any dirt, atmosphere etc. All this will be changed when we get to Umanak and the great communication system breaks down and hunters are found. It seems a very exciting place, the Black Anger tin and zinc mine, the Devil's Thumb. The Skipper, Jonno and I polished off the three-quarter pound of caviar and bottle of champagne, very good it was too.

It rains, is warm, and when it is fine the mosquitos come out. We have all heard about the mosquitos, but I did not believe it till this eve, filling a vast hole in the side of the ship, when whoom! a dozen hard black buggers appear out of the blue and hit everywhere — real caustic bites that have not started to itch after six hours but I reckon they will tomorrow in a big way. One does not expect it in this land — cold, harsh, no life. It has really been quite warm. Down below I am fine at midnight in a short-sleeved sweatshirt and one ragged jersey.

We went and had a meal at the Hotel Godthaab which was very good but too costly, reindeer meat, a great sauce, but ordinary germaine meat. Brian had whale which was apparently slightly fishy and oily, or maybe it was just his onions. The main trouble is that it all comes pre-jarred, pre-packed, airtight-fresh sterilised from Denmark (not the meat of course). I always imagined that this country was self-sufficient, and a little left over for a few tourists and Danes. From what I can gather they export fish, and everything else comes by sea. The tourism is not pushed, which is a good thing, but gimmicky arty things are exported as well, and that's it. Perhaps Godthaab is the exception to all rules. It might be, as it is easily within reach of the outside world. Further north it is impossible even at the best of times to get there. The big boats always come back to the fish factory here, and at the remoter places there are only the indigenous small jobs, mostly hard living. Apparently cod are best caught on a handline dropped to the bottom, lifted up a few feet and jiggled around. Now after our meal Ilan and I are about to start on our letter writing — we talk of college times staying up working all night to get some ridiculously large quantity of work done by breakfast — those days are basically gone — but we will be up for a long time, talking in whispers, drinking, too noisy to make coffee, and the wind howling in this sheltered harbour.

We want to leave tomorrow morning, but if it blows like this straight up the fjord we will never get out till it abates, even right in here we are rocking a lot. We won't be able to do any work on the boat either. We are all going round trying to find the holes where the wet gets in all above the water line, but don't find many of them. I found a rotten patch where I could run my thumb all the way through and about a foot long. I must go to the bank, as none in Umanak, some postcards, stamps and a book or two. It's all very expensive, but they have a few good books. I can't think of any offhand, oh yes, many Tolkien, all the rage here along with Hemingway, although none in English.

Monday, 30th July — It blew hard all last night and in the morning we found ourselves far from where we were with the taffrail wrenched out and the stern generally destroying itself, so I had to set to in rebuilding the transom, and a lot of it was rotten, but a few four-inch nails and coach screws soon fixed it. The boom fitting I also replaced with some alarmingly large coach screws — the whole of that aft section is now held together with the things.

We certainly won't be leaving tonight with this northerly wind, it would be flying in the face of nature. After we had dropped the fisherman and turned the engine on we are now peacefully about ten yards further down wind, the only trouble is getting to and from the jetty or quay or whatever. Brian and Ilan set off and were picked up by a launch from a mile away. It brought them back, landed them on the quay, and Brian started to row back. Half a mile later he was picked up again and this time dumped on the boat. With the oars tied into the rowlocks it's easy enough, with years of experience, that is. The quay is a very interesting structure. The rock is steep to, and there are many fathoms of water till it in any way levels out. The quay is just a wooden frame, or steel frame, bolted into the rock. A whole lot of uprights attached in L-shape to terra firma with vast great logs floating, being able to rise up and down a wire cable, very simple and clever, easy to build, strong, cheap and long-lasting, what could be better. They are dredging all day every day just opposite us to enlarge the harbour facilities to get more and bigger boats in. They are then going to move the factory nearer the larger complex of quays to make it hyper-efficient. Luckily Godthaab cannot expand indefinitely, as it is on a reasonably flat peninsular bounded by the sea on one side and the mountains on the other; neither can the harbour as one is soon into two fathoms of water, so no anchoring and landing fish on shore whatever. No doubt they will find a way to keep this capital of the south, which depends only on the supply ships and fish.

We've left; at four o'clock we went over to the main quay to pick up water and at six we left Godthaab and it's good to be back with the old routine — up at six tomorrow morning, just to shake one's ideas up. As we motor into the sunset the whole coastline stands right out with large patches of snow in the gullies bringing the spurs and crags and exposed faces into perspective — all staggeringly beautiful. If it wasn't for the cold I could sit around and dream just watching them. Luckily one has to go on watch and for two hours if the weather isn't too bad I can gaze to heart's content at the lofty peaks, all great landmarks to navigate by if one can actually see them. It is only on rare days that the sky is not overcast. Apparently all should get better the farther north we go — or south, east or west for that matter. The people here are not as content with life as they can't really achieve anything. There are so many reasonably sophisticated Danes with so little to do. 'Really' seems to have entered my vocabulary in a big way. Everything (another one) seems to be really this and really that. I shall have to go through crossing them all out.

With the engine on we had a really good, quiet read this evening, no one talked. Jonno didn't jabber. Ilan and I had a silent-moves chess run through which was amusing. I am afraid I lost my temper with Jonno this morning. He deserved it. I tried to explain that we weren't all stupid though we may act it. Brian flies off the handle at him as well sometimes. He does so little and complains so much and is really pleased at the first stroke of work he does. I feel in some respects he is like I was last year in the Mediterranean. After a month's sailing you think you know better than anyone else, then you realise you don't. This is perhaps the time when you start to begin to realise what sailing is all about. To live with some other people for a long time at sea can be very grim if there is a nigger in the woodpile, but so often a few people, although inherently totally dissimilar, can get on well with each other. Ilan, Brian and I do. I don't think Harradine would have enjoyed himself, but you never know — he would have quietened things down a bit which would have been the opposite from Jonno and a great change. He's not that bad really. Ilan totally ignores him, Brian and I try our hardest. Ilan has done a good job in collecting a good variety of foods cheaply in this town. Instead of as at Mylor vast quantities of the same thing arriving, there is a great assortment which should last us perhaps till England. The trip is halfway through in time, we must push on a bit, though, in the next few weeks to make up the time lost in Ireland. It was a great pity we missed probably the best month of the year fiddling around waiting.

We ran all last night having motored all the way out of the fjord. The fog descended in the early hours and we have been becalmed all day. This fog is just ridiculous. Always one has to wear oilskins to keep the wet and the mist off, but it helps to keep one warm. My oily trousers are always attached to my boots so I am always either in bunk or oilskins and boots. I have put on another shirt to celebrate our leaving Godthaab. I am going to change all my clothes having had a blissful shower at the Old Man's friends, the Hemmings, but it all seems so pointless so in fact I shall only put on a clean pair of pants and a shirt. My warm socks are wearing out. They don't make them how they used to. My best Lowestoft jersey is on its last legs, the arms are absolutely worn out and the cuffs are on their way out, no doubt I will be able to persuade someone to knit some new sleeves. I'm very fond of it since I was persuaded to buy it for the St John's Ambulance.

August 1st, almost no fog today but overcast. It hardly got dark last night. At midnight you could clearly see the outlines of boats in the distance, and at 3 a.m. it was light enough to read. We passed over Sukkertop bank with many large trawlers anchored and fishing. The Spanish ones *Santa Maria* and *Santa Elisa* were trawling between them going round in a circle. I thought at one stage we were going to be swept into their nets but they got out of our way. Now head winds have plagued us for the last 36 hours, we tack and tack but hardly get anywhere. The current can't be helping us much either. This morning the Old Man was talking of coffee. 'I considered myself an authority on coffee as I farmed it for 15 years in Kenya.' He won 1,000 acres of land at 7,000 feet, on 100 of which he managed to grow coffee to sell in London at £100 a ton, paying the boys 10 shillings a month. He only knew three people out there within about 100 miles — 'It's not good to be on one's own' — and then he met Eric Shipton and they tooled off up Kenya Ruwenzori; then he sold out to Brooke Bond in 1935, was it?, and has been travelling ever since, I suppose. Born in 1898, war till 1918, farmed for 14 years till 1932, climbing in Himalaya till 1939, war till 1945. In 1945 he was 47 years old. Climbing and sailing ever since, I suppose. He probably made a lot of money in Africa.

We tack again at ten and then at 4 p.m. when we have closed the land. The Old Man is very strange about this — presumably he likes to keep well away from land. He always somehow manages to get a good sight in per day even if there is no meridian. We have closed the shore about four times since leaving Godthaab. He gets very worried when he can't identify the coast, assumes it to be so and so from his sometimes dicky sight — very odd for someone of his sort to close the land if he is uncertain of our position when we still have 300 miles to go. 4.30 p.m., the Skipper being on watch, we came to a slow grinding halt, having driven straight over a fishing net, still on head wind now a bit stronger. Panic Stations! Down Sails. What now? O.K. Out come flares (am writing while knowing what comes next) red parachute jobs. How do they work? Read the instructions. It took us about ten minutes in broad daylight and calm sea to get one off, and it flared up about two feet off the sea and was no good. Realised it must have had the stick attached. Let off smoke bomb job, only three instructions this time. (1) Rip off top (2) Pull string (3) Throw in water to leeward. To our delight orange smoke poured out. We could hardly see it but I suppose an aircraft could if looking hard. Good firework display anyway. Boat comes over, has a look, drops a lifeboat, two toughs drop down, and pull net out. Boat comes to windward, drops line, pulls us out. They couldn't speak English but didn't seem angry at all that their nets were torn and buggered up, I suppose they have to get used to loss, but they were all good new nets. All the other Greenlanders still tidying up other nets, mending unconcerned, bare-handed in oilskins. We were right close in-shore which did not help with a reef about half a mile away. Why not keep out to sea, and have some sea room and out of the banks and boats.

Friday 3rd. August — At 2.30 the Old Man headed back to shore. On my watch at about 5 a.m. I came across a boat, went to leeward of it and started working up to windward again behind it and came upon a danbuoy, then another smaller one. O.K. bear away. Then another one, bear away again, and another and another and another. Ah, we should be able to get through that gap (I was westing at this stage, trusting about south-east) no, another danbuoy — head to wind through wind, everything backed — hands out into the open, very cold wet gear — get her sailing again — back along the line of nets and out to sea — hands absolutely frozen. Off watch at six; just crawling into bunk when Skipper wakes 'What the hell are we on this tack for?' My entry in the log was 'Abundance of boats, nets, buoys, lines.' Out on deck again, off we go near-hauled, freezing cold. Skipper comes on watch at 8 a.m. We were just finishing breakfast when he shouted

'Below'. He had driven over another net, Oh dear! More wind this time, about Force 3 N.N.W. Down sails, Oh dear! he's done it again (why not stay out at sea?). Slowly we pull the net into a complete bight. We drift onto another, round the prop on top of the other. All hands, off goes the parachute, this time with wooden stick out of the exhaust pipe. No result. Off goes smoke flare. We are getting into the hang of these things. No result. The third flare produced the Eldorado (Norwegian) whose nets they were. They contrived a great plan, got hold of another boat, then they changed places and the second boat towed us for a bit; nothing happened, so we started to chop and chop away. We came free at about 12.30 with two ropes round the prop and 15 feet four times top and bottom trailing astern from the two nets. We got the sails up (wind Force 4) and off we went to seaward — he starts signalling us on the Aldis — no result, no one is looking, too busy tidying up the mess on deck. He comes alongside. 'Go eastwards' so off we tack and get her in stays. O.K. jybe her round. People frantically waving from the bridge, two danbuoys to leeward of us. Round she goes, eastward we go. 'You're 24 miles from Sukkertop' is all he says. We have lunch, me on watch, till 2.00. Ilan comes on, and at 2.30 there's a buoy ahead. Out of bunk, but it's only a boat. 4.30 the action starts again, to go about and reef. We go about and reef, drop jib, get wet again up to the elbows on both sides. Helm hard over, we loose her, try to jybe her round, she won't come. Tack her round, she won't go, try again, round she goes, helm hard over. Skipper on watch. We leave block in stay-sail, and nearly lose her twice more. It must be the junk underneath holding her to windward. She's eased off now, but it's still Force 4. We might just be making north of true west. We had the only good thing of the day for supper, a beautiful 6lb. salmon retrieved from the net before the boat came over.

At 8.30 a trawler bears down on us — Oh help, what's up now? Red over white over white on foremast, panic stations, she came right close up to windward. We waved, they waved. All O.K. just having a look, thank the Lord for that. We could do without any more of these traumas for the day. I'm really whacked although I feel alright on watch from 10 to midnight, still light. If I can survive that watch we should be out of the area by six tomorrow morning. I wish this wind would stop, head winds are much worse than calms, I reckon. They are either too light to make to windward or too strong. First it was too light, now it's too strong. Oh well, one doesn't go to sea for nothing. I wish to God the Old Man would keep out to sea in these conditions, I think I would.

He did something yesterday that surprised me for about four seconds, because I would have been too late. After we had cleared the net we saw a line of seaweed with a ball on a bit of it. Brian was convinced that it was a net, but I thought it was alright. We were now beating parallel to it. Bear away quick, says the Skipper. Helm hard over, I let out the mainsheet still not realising, and we passed to seaward at right angles. Just before he spoke, I realised. 'It might have been a reef.' Well, luckily we didn't touch anything. 'If you're going to hit anything, do it straight on.'

Another day, and we're still on headwind, we made nothing to the north all night, and after breakfast tacked to about N.E. true. Almost at the Arctic Circle and we prepare for a small celebration. The Old Man talked at breakfast about appearing as Borealis with Brian as his wife and initiating us all. We won't make it today, though, 66.08° at midday. This north wind is a bore now. It must have got quite a current going as well but now shows signs of abating, but not changing direction. Ilan's Christmas pudding and my wine must wait until tomorrow, or the day after, or we might never get there. We dare not heave to for fear of losing ground. At the moment we must just be making. I was very touched yesterday by the Old Man offering me his best and only precious yellow bobble hat. During the net changing procedure I was all over the side trying to keep dry and cut the netting when I felt my bobble hat go. I reached up, grasped it and threw it straight over the other side to the pleasure of the fishing. They cheered, I dashed over, boathook in hand, but just missed. Worst thing of a bad day. Ilan has just given me his Greek lambswool one which is much better, but I dropped that over when tacking after breakfast. Luckily we were stationary and I grabbed it on the second attempt. One has to wear some sort of headwear even under oilskins to stop one's forehead catching this cold wind. If it can be used to cover the ears as well one's a lucky person. A balaclava is good but it slips upwards easily and therefore is no real use.

The wick in the fire came to a grinding halt yesterday, a great yellow flare coming up. The wick had burnt right away and had to be bastardised to increase its length, which I managed successfully. We still have the worry of the net round the prop and miles of it still trailing behind us. We can cut the stuff off the prop under calm, but the stuff caught in the rudder and keel band never. I shall try attaching a lump of ballast to bits of it to try that way.

Sunday 5th — The wind got up in the night to about Force 6. We still manage to point about 45° off the wind and are even making to the north, most amazing really. It is easing off now the glass is going up. No doubt it will start raining again soon as the front passes, or whatever fronts do round here. The *Pilot* paints a hopeless picture of everything. The weather is foggy, cloudy, many gales, head winds for summer. In winter only the temperature gets worse, everything else gets better, except the hours of sunshine, that is. Last night was cold and wet. We were on the wrong tack, starboard, so that the drips got inside my leeboard. I cover myself up in my space-blanket always now and the sleeping-bag completely when not in it. Last night there was a quarter of a pint of water in a ruck in the space-blanket just near the edge about to topple into the bag. Luckily it takes time to permeate the bag and one's clothes on entry so one can usually get to sleep in the time, but waking up is a bit of a nightmare, it's just like a hothouse. It makes it reasonably pleasurable to get up, which is the only consolation. The wind might have backed a little.

We crossed the Circle probably this afternoon sometime. Not a very impressive place, this Arctic. Feet were quite cold on watch, but not nearly as bad as the night near Farewell. We have made about 20 miles in the last day which can't be bad considering an average Force 6/7 all the time. We had a celebratory dinner, whisky, corned beef, mushrooms, Christmas Pud and a magnum of Spanish claret, mine. Pretty good at it's price. We all feel really content and full, the simple pleasures in life. This meal is a great change, what one might have on land and therefore just as good if not better. I polished off *Valparaiso* by Nicolas Freeling in an afternoon — very bad. The Old Man has now awakened, straining to read by the light of an oil-lamp. I have now almost finished *Flight to Arras*. It's just like *Terre des Hommes* roughly translated as Wind, Sand and Stars. I don't appreciate his style. Pseudo-philosophy mixed up with good thrilling flying wartime France stories. He thinks an awful lot of himself, great priest, great brain. He could get across a far better picture if he wrote more descriptions of what life and flying were like in France in 1940, not by describing it in abstract terms. It's probably just me and my liking for concrete things, and not being able to understand what he's trying to convey. The language is very stilted, no doubt that's the translator trying to be absolutely accurate.

Monday, August 6th — Wind down to Force 3 but still dead ahead. We have been making about 25 miles a day to the north, slow and not too sure. Holsteinborg is on the beam and another fishing bank ahead. The fog came down last night and didn't clear till 10 a.m., and now the sun is out and it is pleasant to be on the deck even if it is a bit cold. My salmon line is out in the hope and the net still with us. I have been conniving dreadful schemes for removing the stuff from the keel band, with a knife attached to a pole. It must come off the keel band because the floating stuff is so long that it is catching in the propellor. One might be able to do it but perhaps not so. I didn't sleep much last night as we tacked at 10 p.m., and I was on watch from 2 till 4, we tacked again at 4, to sleep at 5, up at 7.30, and the sun is enervating if soporific. I have been running around putting whippings on the staysail sheets, as the ends were all going to buggery. Now I'm about to start the romantic fantasy of *The Go-Between*, it should be good.

Tuesday now, and we were becalmed all last night drifting with the tide God knows where. Islands and land appeared suddenly out of the clouds, most of them unidentifiable. We are not sure about using the engine, it should be alright but now we have a wind — no guesses where from — north all the way from the Pole it feels. No doubt we will be starting this tacking business all over again. We are now heading for the land, why I don't know. The Old Boy thinks we get much further to the north doing N.E. by E. than N.W. by W. Hard cold work for us. We will no doubt be tooling around the great Helskinnoss bank soon getting caught up in nets again. Oh well, all good fun except we are running desperately short of time.

Last night he was telling us about bathing naked in the Serpentine. It all started from our industrious work getting the rope off the prop and Jonno wanting to dive in and hack away. He was dissuaded luckily. In this club in Dover Street, apparently, one was allowed to swim starkers before eight o'clock in winter. He used to run from Dover Street, swim and run back. One day in the fog he heaved himself out to find himself on the wrong side, and had to run all the way round over the bridge and back to his clothes, a good sight. Also on one Arctic voyage he had a competition before breakfast — 3 bucketfuls of water over one — who could last longest. He managed to Cape

Farewell but the other guy did another 30 days. In the days when I was stronger, he recalls. Also all of the cranks at the Serpentine, the man who used to wear his gloves to break the shock as he dived in, the other who ran in the wet grass because the dew was good for his feet. It all sounded very amusing, especially when he burst out laughing pushing his yellow bobble hat right forwards till it was up to his eyebrows so he had to peer up at one. At other times he has it pushed right back which when he's got his glasses on makes him look wizened and professional. He is in a way, I suppose. He disbelieves anything he can't see himself. The worry about being able to see the sun when it is below the horizon and the wash basin. Now you can't see the plughole. Fill it with water — now you can. All very difficult. I don't really believe it, especially as the term horizon is said in the dictionary to mean the line at which earth and sky *appear* to meet. Not where they actually do meet if one is six feet off the ground. We assume that light travels in straight lines. It does but its path can take the line of a curve so that when one sees the sun above the horizon then it is above the horizon. It must be, even though the rays of the sun are bent, reflective, refractions etc.

The wind has got up again from the north and we fight once more. We had trouble this morning trying to find out where the hell we were. Islands in the Stream all moving engloomed. We did not really manage to identify any of it. We took hundreds of sights and hope for the best. It doesn't really matter at this stage, just stops us sleeping well. It will drive us round the bend. Our night in Hades will be fighting against the everlasting borealis.

We now for once know exactly where we are, just north of Holsteinborg, making almost no progress with this Force 3 head wind. The mountains are clear and staggering, scraps of snow in the gulleys with pinnacles all around. The sun is out and there should be a great sunset. Luckily I am on watch to midnight. It has been really warm today by comparison, and I did not need to keep my hands in my duvet pockets. I hope we will dry out soon then I won't need to wear my oilskins' trousers. It should come by rights. When we tack at ten we will head off almost into the sun. Is Brazil larger than Australia? Ilan and I have a bet on it. Brian reckons with me yes. 3.1 million square miles for Australia, about 3.3 for Brazil I reckon. I remember looking it up and being surprised. One small thing that is troubling us is what is the name of the first letter of the old manuscripts and scrolls. Rubric?

The compasses seem to be all up the creek so we must start taking sights and timings and make up a deviation card of sorts. Will have to do it off the H.B.C. and transfer it to the ship's one approximately.

Wednesday, 8th August — Light same wind with fog. What else is there to say? It epitomises the whole atmosphere on the boat, fog. I suppose we are getting used to it. Quarter to six, there is a boat blowing its top. It has hardly moved in half an hour. Perhaps a naval one, because they seem to be the only people who really reduce speed to match visibility. They can't get far in these waters. We had a go at chopping away the net this morning. Highly unsuccessful in chopping but we did manage to pick up the last trailing strand and have now got the boathook caught in it. It means that it is perfectly safe now to use the engine which is comforting, if it starts. The old beast is slowly falling to pieces but as yet has never failed us.

Thursday, 9th August — Becalmed at midnight. Started the engine after breakfast, stopped to try and cut off boathook and broke boathook no. 2. Land has been beautifully in sight all day. In the early morning all the colours were showing in the mountains. This is what the Arctic should be. It was light all last night and it is almost very clear now. Disko might be in sight. We have to make it to this Island about 50 miles from Umanak to meet a friend of the Old Man's, Dr Drever, a geologist from St Andrews, but he leaves on the 14th though. They have a hut up there and a few grads and curious professors come and stay there studying mountains, water, ice and so on. Let's hope we arrive in time, it should be an interesting collection of people. I suggest too that we take over their hut for the winter and stay up here. For want of something better to do Ilan and I are planning to make a tray for his cakes and pastries. I suggest:

THE

BAROQUE

1973

Have just floated a bottle message which reminded the Old Man of a Chilean whaler who caught an albatross and tied a message to its leg saying position, number of whales, etc. It was shot a year later 3,000 miles away.

Friday, 10th August, becalmed almost all of last night. The engine started pouring smoke, as it always does, but worse today. Between 2 and 4 I took the exhaust manifold off, and found the end bolts sheered off and the gaskets to buggery. Would you believe it, we had two spares! The other owner must have had the same problem; but it was no better for the moment. When I restarted her blue smoke started pouring out, then she ran hot. The Old Man said 'It's worse than the bloody war.' I thought I had made a balls of it, so tightened everything up and so there's almost no leaking for the time being. There is still a gentle headwind, but we have forgotten that. We have spent so much time trying to get here so we might as well make certain of it as time is getting short. There was a most incredible sunrise. All the preliminaries, a crimson fluorescent streak broadening and brightening to north-east, then much brighter in the middle, starting to flame red and with a touch of yellow, then the orb appeared. I looked at it through the sextant, very pretty pantechnicolour, half one colour, half another. Temperature up to 10° and a great pleasure to be on deck. The engine leaking oil, and I put in 3 pints today, there must be a simple answer.

Saturday, and one lead off the dynamo and oil pressure gauge are leaking, I fixed both. Exhaust deck fitting shook loose, burnt the deck. We were running her at 2,000 revs, obviously too much, everything rattled off. The water outlet pipe gave way, steam and water hissed out — there's a piece of string round it now. There's not much more that can go wrong that I can repair. Tappits, yes. I must remember to check the oil. The Old Man now thinks like me about meeting with this Drever guy, not really meaning to see him but we might as well as we're now so near. We were back in the ice yesterday, two large bergs and quite a few bits, it breaks the horizon wonderfully. It felt like being back at home, being in ice again. Another great sunrise this morning, straight and proper, a brilliant yellow orange sphere rising over the horizon burning down on one; from 4 to 6 I was outside in a thin pair of trousers and no oilskins. I wonder when I will next be able to do a dawn watch without oilskins, next year?

It's Saturday night, whisky tot time. Every Saturday, some Sundays, a week in the North and a few other odd occasions. When the Old Man's on his own or people are aboard out comes the booze. In Godthaab he would always have one of a night and twice he had a smaller one at lunch time. Once I appeared just as he was emptying the whisky into a glass, about four fingers of it, and he had to offer me some. He wanted to but just didn't know how to say it properly.

I've just finished *The Magus*, having half read it before. It was very much better this time, I became totally involved with it at some stages. It goes on far too long though and is really a nothingness. Fowles' imagination is desperately fired; he starts off promisingly about the school, the people, Alison, the idea of it all, then it becomes desperate. He has an imagination, a good one, but had to continue the story as if indefinitely to make it long and look complicated, when he was only trying to put forward an idea, a concept of play, theatre, charade — not masque, that sounds too formal. He is mistaken though about the Molkino blowing from the Ionian Islands. It comes from the Turkish coast southwards. A devastating wind of great force rather like the Mistral Bora.

Yesterday and this morning we could have been in the Med., that deep wine-dark sea. Only the mountains needed changing and the ice of course. In fact the mountains were O.K. There was snow on the Albanian ones in October with the sun shining, only my friendly desert island is ice. I presume a piece of melting glacier can be a friend even though you know it will dissolve. Some life it would be, perhaps thirty years, travelling from one side of Greenland to the other through the world. I shall wait till I get back to England before I start reading about the Arctic, I don't feel like doing it now. I want to get a feel of the place first. I found this with the Med. I had ample opportunity to read about it when there, but it wasn't as real as after. If I had read *Ulysses* before having been to some of the places it would have meant nothing.

Back to the mundane. We will probably push on to this island, Obungat, motoring to perhaps midnight. I suppose the Old Man has never motored at night. Naive, isn't it. He has no faith in engines, not surprisingly as he has never had a decent one. Even the Rolls Royce in the boat they chartered gave up on them, though Colin Putt was on board. This was in the Antarctic, and they packaged the whole gubbins off at Australia and an identically similar one returned. I have absolute faith in good engines. I remember Alan Cowley's on *Ezra Pound*. Black enamel, second best. The top ones are white enamel so that any spot of oil would show. I think of Geoffrey's so-called engine room, how proud he was of it, painting, oiling caressing from dawn to dusk, it still gave up on him. I am getting rather fond of this old rattling Ford. It looks and sounds as if it is about to fall through the bottom of the boat, the bearers are as rotten as hell and all the coach bolts just turn and turn. I have succumbed at last to my long underpants. No doubt they will make all the difference.

Monday, motored all night till 4 this morning. On watch 10–12. Ran into a lot of nets at one o'clock and spent the next hour manoeuvring out of them. Disko is looking very fine. Sandstone cliffs, green slopes, and snow on mountains when the cloud clears. With luck at this rate we will be at Igdlorssuit tomorrow evening, to leave a day of friendship with Dr Drever. We are running short on literature, only the detectives and a few others left. With luck, we will be able to scrounge a lot out of Drever's lot. The Old Boy's really grumpy. I, just awake, didn't help the others tack at midday, and he asked why the hell I couldn't give a hand. Because no one asked, that's why. He was a bit red in the face and can't stand Jonno.

It is another ninety miles to Igdlorssuit and another fifty or so to Umanak, then we must think of going home. Sad so much for perhaps so little. The next four days will be the climax of the voyage — let's hope they are. We got almost up to 70° North, 1,200 miles to go. Ellesmere is another 400 miles north. It would really have taken a long time to get there, the Old Man reckons one ought to leave in May. We started motoring again at 4 p.m. and will no doubt continue for the last sixty miles to get us in at midday or so tomorrow. We will not be stopped now. There are icebergs all around, more than there have ever been; all the chisel shapes are incredible. We went and took a look at a very large one, about 400 feet long, 50 feet high. As we passed round it we found it to be joined to another underwater. The shapes and curves are ever changing, like a kaleidoscope, jagged edges appearing, melting into graceful curves with large pinnacles about to fall off, with deep blue fault lines. We saw a little pack iceberg some way away, and a seal which we thought to be ice. One evening a few days ago we were drifting at about 7 p.m. when I was standing just aft of the gallows when I heard a slight movement of water. I looked down to see a face, innocent and doglike, peering up at me, whiskers bristling. He/she then proceeded to drift around mainly with head above water, sometimes diving. They all have such a pained expression on their faces — must be the cold. It's a pity the sun doesn't come out. It would make the voyage, to be in really close in brilliant sunshine, with our shirts off and sunhats. If time permits we should be in Umanak glacier, I would like that, to see where the ice comes from. From all our navigation we reckoned that we would pass the northern tip of

Hare at about 7.30 p.m. At 7.30 Jonno appears — land dead ahead with fjord type running east. It must be the channel between Hare Island and Disko. No, it can't be, it's too narrow. Where is it then? Dig out all the charts. Only place possible is Disko Fjord 40 miles to the south. Yesterday's meridian proves opposite. On we go. It looks only three miles across at most, we all agree. Two valleys on the right, pictures estimate of lots of mountains. Fog opening to the east, we turn out in case it is a fjord. It can't be, impossible, it must be, it has to be. A deciding argument. It must have been a westerly gale to blow us in this far. On we go. Six cross bearings agree. It's still impossible to believe we have six miles between us and the coast. Very many deep vertical fissures, I've never seen anything like it.

We saw some basking sharks, vast animals, looking like enormous porpoises with a much larger dorsal fin. Divers, black and little auks, and Ilan trying to go to sleep with engine going, almost an impossibility. We all slept this afternoon and this morning too because of last night, but I doubt if we will have a chance tomorrow — who knows — I suppose the engine will be running again. We've enough fuel to get us all the way to Umanak, just.

Here we are at Ubekendt and it's another 18 miles to Igdlorssuit, so we'll be there at 3 p.m. or thereabouts and with luck just find Drever. It has been raining all the morning and there is much ice. Ubekendt seems to be composed mainly of shale. The Cornvist Pass is really old and covered with a curious faultline fathom, there are two grey and yellow wide bands, one running almost horizontally and the other covering it at about 35° — weird — while the main faultlines are on the line bisecting this angle. 'Where the air is radio-active, Oh the wild west is where I want to be.'

Tuesday, and we were given a royal welcome yesterday by the Greenlanders, Dr Drever, Frank George and son and a New Zealander. Flare sent up and they gave us char and whalemeat, which we had for dinner. They left at about seven o'clock, so we only made it by a few hours. It was pretty astonishing to talk to these people in such a deserted place, but they talk of the area favourably. Alpine type mountains, salmon fishing, mamordile mines, the fjords, glaciers, everything. Drever has been coming to Igdlorssuit since 1937 apparently, and knows and loves the island well. George is the secretary of the Institute of Navigation. His name rings a bell somewhere. He knows all about geology anyway, and told us that the rock round Adho looks like this for what that is worth. This large settlement consists of about 25 houses, old men and children, what they all do I can't imagine. There is a small whaling boat, and shark skins are hanging up drying. Another man, David Meldrum, will appear, who is second in command of the base apparently. We hope to scrounge some food and literature off him, although I don't think he will want to part with these expensive items. We are on the lookout for drifting bergs, there are some near us but the sound is chock full of them. The sun is about to rise over them and the Alpine mountains. We had whale meat last night and it was quite filling, tasted of liver with the consistency of poor meat, I didn't particularly enjoy it but it is apparently better than seal. Drever produced a wet suit for the Old Man which is very curious. I shall have to try it out, I suppose, though I don't think even a wet suit would do much for one against this water. What's really interesting at the moment is that for about a quarter of an hour it is very pleasant on deck at lunch in two pairs of trousers, shirt and jersey. After that the cold sets in. Even so it is very pleasurable because of what goes with it. The huskies that line the banks howl all night. One starts, they all start. Then quiet. This place is built on the slight green slope between sea and stone mountains. It is on a small bay of black sandy shale, and the visibility is amazing. At last we are having Arctic weather. We could easily see Umanak mountain 50 miles away. The sun is about to appear over the mountain tops. It has taken nearly two hours to go from the crimson radiance to the now orange brilliance. A loud roaring noise wakes me from my thoughts. Two hundred yards away a soft iceberg breaks in half; a vast chunk shears off the topside, slides into the water almost submerged. The other part lifts perhaps fifteen feet up, then down as the sheared-off bit rises and falls and both settle to their new levels, small wavelets beat the shore and the boat wakes.

We are invited to a Kaffenik this morning, which is the social life around here. We don't know where, but the flags will probably be out as they are on Sundays and peoples' birthdays. I have spent all this morning doing minor repairs and now we're going out.

On Monday I set off up the mountain. I was just going for a stroll with Ilan but he did not want to go on after a bit so I went on on my own. I had spoken to John the geologist who explained how terrible the rock is but that a St Andrews party had made it up this gap. So off I went out, rope and compass in hand. I soon became enmeshed, not wanting to continue and not able to retreat. Five and half hours later I scrambled finally with utter relief to the top. Twice I thought I would never make it. Twice I had forced myself on because I knew I had to. I was stupid really. John had said, 'I don't want to offer advice' and he was obviously relieved when I appeared back at 9.30. By the beach I met this guy David Meldrum who is doing something with Manchester University. He has been up here four or five times and will probably come out with us for a few days and show us round. We will pinch a whole lot of stores from St Andrews hut when they leave. David works with the Greenland Geophysicist Society — might be able to get a job with them perhaps. We think we will leave tomorrow. I was very tired after yesterday. I knew that if I hadn't been fit I would never have made it. With any luck David and I will get a chance to do at least one good climb on Umanak.

Tuesday, 14th August — Spent all morning fiddling around trying to get the netting off. We leaned the boat over, I went over the side in the dinghy and chopped it all off about two feet below the water line. Some got wrapped round the prop shaft in the process which didn't help. Jonno took the tiller apart again in an effort to curb its curious behaviour. We don't leave today, perhaps tomorrow. Just after lunch we all went to a Kaffenik. A great Greenland invention, you just go along to this guy's house, there's a sign outside saying welcome and you laugh and smile and everybody likes you. They are all very friendly and the language barrier is no great problem, although they and you will not have had a clue of what has happened. John, David and John our translators had a hard time interpreting 'We sent up two rockets when Dr Drever left.' It produced 'The Germans have put their first satellite into orbit.' (The Postillion has been struck by lightning.) Jonno and Ilan went off to this dance for a change and came back saying all very good and the young girls all dolled to the eyebrows. There are almost no young men and no middle-aged people — gone off leaving hundreds of very friendly children who follow you around everywhere, and are fantastic with boats and always willing to lend a hand but they get bored doing anything. It's odd here that all summer the people do nothing and in the winter and spring they hunt and collect food. Their kayaks are fantastically light and are able to be rowed swiftly. They are very light skin on wood — no nails or screws. It would be great to spend a winter with these people to see them at a time when you can't just walk down to the shop and buy anything and the only way to travel is by sledge. All the huskies are either chained apart so they can't fight or just let loose around the place. They hardly fight and take no interest except in sleeping and eating. Attractive looking animals but how they can move once they get going.

Wednesday, 15th August — Left Igdlorssuit at about midday having spent the morning helping David clear up his gear and get fuel for his zoner etc. Motored down to the southern tip of Upernivik Island and are now anchored just off the mainland to the south of Upernivik. All the mountains around are spectacular and impressive although they don't look very high. Almost all the peaks are over 6,000 feet. David and I have planned to set off at first light to gain the icecap by way of any easy couloir and then do a peak to try it out. It will be a long day and my first taste of Alpine climbing. Not technically difficult, just an awful lot of it. I am writing this at one in the morning in a place totally enclosed by mountains. It is unfortunately not quite light enough for my light meter to register as all the outlines of the mountains are very clear and sharp.

Thursday, 16th August — Seem to have missed a day in the counting.

Friday, 17th August — David, the Old Man, Ilan and I left for Upernivik two miles inland; away at nine o'clock. The Old Man had a 4–5,000 foot peak in mind. Ilan wandered off. David and I set off for the 2,000 foot base of the larger couloir. By 2.00 p.m. we were at the top of it, realising how unfit we were. David was here in 1967 with this St Andrews party and knew his way around. It was a struggle on the imperfect snow, but we saw the sun on the high mountains all around.

I was feeling pretty shattered by this time anyway. We then decided to go for Mount Change 5.00 p.m. Three hours later we were out of the rocks and life became easier. At 8.00 p.m. I stood on the summit, the first person to reach the top of the peak from sea-level. The view was staggering. We were both tired and unfit and knew we had to do six hours descent after 10 hours of continuous hard going. It took seven hours to get back to the sea. The couloir was frozen up and I did most of it on my arse as I fell quite a few times on it and only stopped myself with dextrous use of my ice axe. It was bloody cold. I was exhausted but I had enjoyed myself. We got back to the boat by four o'clock after 19 hours continuous exercise — quite a feat, I thought. The rock climbing was very much exposed but not difficult. Coffee and whisky at 4.30 with the Old Man. He reckoned that we ought to have been back by midnight and had been reckoning that we would take twelve hours.

Slept till lunch time and recovered. Did nothing all a.m. David left. We should leave tomorrow morning for Umanak.

On way to Umanak. Hope to get a go at this 3,000 foot mountain which has been climbed twice before. But according to the St Andrews party it is hard going, all on rock (according to Brian the north side is a pretty barren place). I expect there is a way up. It looks an attractive climb from a distance but as there is no snow it may not attract the mountaineers. 3,000 feet of difficult rock would take a long time but be amusing. One island we passed on the way from Upernivik had a 3,000 foot climbable-looking crack, fine exposure and sustained, one might call it. The weather is slowly breaking up, which might provide a good excuse for not doing Umanak. After that we are homeward bound with probably a stop somewhere in the south — no doubt a lot more motoring till we get there if the engine holds out. We've filled up with diesel and watched the ice get nearer and nearer the harbour entrance. We had to move once to get out of the way of one piece. A good southerly wind is blowing to get us round the promontory fifty miles away.

Anchor watch all last night, a very beautiful one, the moonlight on the mountains and bergs. Quite a few have blown into the harbour and it looked at 4 a.m. as if we wouldn't get away, still the southerly wind blowing in. After breakfast when we intended to leave there was still a small exit through the ice. We had a go, slipped off the wind and nearly lost the boat on the rocks. How the Old Man stands the strain I don't know. After lunch we got a tow out nearly running into a few pieces, and we are now on our way west with very unpleasant seas — no wind, calm then a squall. We've got the log line wrapped round the keel band but all otherwise bright, sunny and hot, jybing, tacking, and manoeuvring round bergs. At 2.15 this morning I set off to post some letters and was raped as I stepped ashore. A girl of about 18 smelling of drink came up, leant against me and stared into my eyes. A little exciting except for the possible aftermath of screaming from the quay and a dose of the clap.

John Elder the geologist from Igdlorssuit is in Umanak and left about the same time as we did, getting back to England in 17 hours' time. We leave the Arctic in all its splendour behind us. It's very sad to be leaving after such a short time considering the three months it took us to get here. England will no doubt be damp and gloomy, the Channel worst of all probably. I must start seriously considering what will follow next, perhaps a trip down to the Antarctic with the Old Man. Ilan will come and perhaps Angus Clarke if he's doing nothing else.

Another good warm day. Seven feet of the log line is now wrapped round the prop shaft which doesn't help and it's not quite calm enough to get at it. We are becalmed now but have had a few scattered hours of good sailing to get us past this first promontory before we can turn south. It looks as if we will be without a log line soon. Jonno scared us out of our wits at six o'clock this morning by starting the engine to get us out of the way of a berg. One imagines that one's last minutes are at hand. We all dashed up on deck — no boots this time.

Now the weather is breaking up. We have motored most of today and Disko still looks the same distance away in the same direction. My boots have decided to give up their fight for existence by splitting just at the turn of foot to leg on the upper side — so much for Mr Dunlop's new best. I shall try sewing and canvas patching and everything else as my others are too small for comfort. I seem to be running out of steam and the content is becoming less wordy and more factual and generally more boring. When we start sailing again I reckon things will start improving. Life is just empty at the moment as we are heading south. It probably will feel like this till we pass Farewell again. Only a month now till my 21st, luckily no celebrations for me I hope — perhaps no one will know or remember. What a romantic and melancholy idea.

It's still sunny and we're sailing now, running comfortably at a knot and a half. Midday only 5°C. Nothing much happening on board. In the evening we're now running at 3 knots, getting better and better. The Old Man is playing patience. Tomorrow and we're running for our lives at $4\frac{1}{2}$ knots, reefed right down, going like a battle axe. We will be swept out of the Davis Straight like a dose of salts at this rate. Another three days of this and we will have broken the back of our homeward voyage, one more day of it will be a good step. It is very exhilarating sailing and the watches go quickly, if cold.

Sunday, and we spent all last night on double watches because we ran into the remains of the Middle Pack. It took us almost to nightfall to work out what all the ice was and it was late by the time we tumbled to it. First we hove to, then took all the sails down and lay a-hull; we kept on having to start the engine to get out of the way of ice — we ran into one bit which has left a large scar. I got to sleep at 10.30, up at midnight till 5, up at 7.30, sleep at midday to 5.30 p.m.; by this time the wind had died right down, from very nearly gale force to about Force 2 and we are now running S.E. with full main.

On Monday the wind is starting to get up again, it's now about Force 4 with the glass steady and still we run on eating up the miles effortlessly. One thing we should have spotted yesterday was the water temperature going down to freezing for the first time, it was our longest coldest night of the voyage so far. I am surprised we have not had more long nights. The tiller is playing up again, much worse than before, we'll be lucky if it lasts long enough to get us home.

Well that didn't last long, we ran into a full S.E. gale, and on my watch I heard this great crack and had to go and tell the Old Man that the boom had sprung. We got the sail down and I'll try to get it off on my next watch, if the wind has dropped. All good clean fun and I'll chalk it up to experience. The blow is over now and we are running under jib, staysail and one of the old jibs lashed up to the mast — it is old and rotten but not as rotten as the first one we tried, as soon as there was any tension it started to tear; a child of two could have torn it into dishcloths. There's still quite a sea running. We set the staysail and the comic jib on the mast and averaged one knot. It took me four strenuous hours to recover the peak halyard and shackle on the port topping lift. We are still making too much water for anybody's liking, about 700 pumps an hour. We have rolled on the whole roll of wire onto the boom, which has sprung about four feet from the after end, and lashed on a long piece of steel. Five or six hours work, and we are all very tired. The staysail tore just before breakfast and the main just after it was set loose-footed. The next day we put a jacket over the wire serving on the boom and bent on the mainsail and now we are on our way again. The wind has backed, high cirrus clouds this morning, yellow sunset last night — it can only mean one thing: the barometer will start falling. With a lot of luck the wind might go right round and blow from the west. I have very nearly fallen asleep on watch these last few nights. It was good yesterday, when we had the mainsail up loose-footed for ten minutes before it tore and the decks were clear, we could sit down and relax and look at it. Now at 10.30 we have everything under control, and we sit in the saloon reading and writing. I'll go now and photograph some of the damage.

★

The times of writing are getting fewer and fewer as more happens. On Friday the wind backed to S.E. as expected, and by midnight we were reefed down and going reasonably well, doing just north of east. This is when it started to rain and hardly stopped for three days. All Saturday the wind increased and we started the double watch after supper with wind Force 6 and all seemed to be steady. Jonno and I were rudely awakened halfway through our four hours' respite and down came all sails, and at 4 in the morning we sat round drinking coffee and three-quarters of a bottle of very cheap rum — at least there was no need for the double watch — it was a very tiring night; by Monday morning we were utterly becalmed and rolling round like an old pig waiting for something to happen. We motored 18 miles on Monday, at which the fog arrived and stayed till Tuesday afternoon; by then we had destroyed the gearbox, which now makes the engine totally unusable. The nut holding the main ball race had come undone, it was red hot and had no oil in it, and the guard was all buggered up — still it's easily repairable given a stable platform, the manual and perhaps some spare parts. Oh well, we don't really need it now, we're not so far from home. Just before supper we made a futile attempt to sail, but without luck until at 00.20 this morning there was a breeze from the S.W. so we upped all sails, and moved about three miles during the night. The wind has steadily backed and increased, now at Force 3/4; I think we will celebrate when a westerly comes. It's not that we aren't trying to get south, we just can't. We make E. by S. at the moment, about right for Liverpool, it's all very depressing, in the last ten days we have made no more than 100 miles towards home and it's all so uncomfortable, it's either too cold or too wet to work on deck — though mind you nothing like the Davis Strait. At least now all self-supporting pieces of steel can be held onto almost indefinitely without actual pain. We are now running short of food, water, paraffin and almost everything else. Jonno's voice is just as painful and boring, the Old Man up the wall, we are all pretty grumpy to think that we did the first 600 miles, that we thought would be the worst, in a week, and now we fight for even due east. These S.E. winds can't last for ever, I suppose, but I am beginning to doubt it. The glass has hardly shifted for that last lot, for five days we have prayed for a change up or down, but no — rock steady. Now the wind increases and we reef down. Double watches and all this sleep problem and we just keep going from one meal-time to the next. The wind this time is from S.S.E. Let's hope that is a trend southwards and clockwise, but I shall believe these westerlies only when I feel them. At least now we are making reasonable progress if painfully. I can imagine people saying 'You must have had an easy if perhaps rough passage going east'; rough yes, but not easy. These last two times I have been on 8–10 p.m. which means 8 to midnight, 4–8 a.m. and then 12–2 p.m. If this goes on much longer we shall have to have a more efficient system and swap over with collaborated meal-times etc., or an electric pump with battery charging every day or so, since we have all this redundant diesel and petrol and lack of paraffin. It seems ridiculous and ironical to have abundance of one thing and severe lack of another. We are certainly not going to be able to tolerate any gear failure, sickness or anything else. I haven't slept well these last few days, worked hard, gone round finding things to do, tidying up this, making that. I feel I have lost Ilan's interest slightly; perhaps that's just an inferiority complex, in that one is so much aware of any intense feelings. These long hours we are putting in will cure this to a great extent — so much more to do and less time to think — more mistakes, the possibility of short rations. Head winds don't exactly help matters, this is almost the same sort of weather we had part of the way up, though stronger. I never realised how quickly we made the passage from Ireland to Farewell, about 18 days for the 1,200 or so miles. Now I look forward to getting back to Lymington with all its boats and trains, a great contrast and relief. At sea I am procrastinating — have I time to steal?

Where was I now? It has rained continuously and blown from the S.E. till we hove to early last Friday. By lunch time with a rapidly falling barometer we were becalmed, then very soon a breeze came from the west, the skies showed signs of clearing, and we were on the move again. Now, on Saturday, the wind is from the N.W. and increasing slightly to Force 4. We can't as yet make the course but we are comfortable at last. The Old Man got his sight after a week which put us on course. A large Russian trawler came over and asked if we wanted anything. We asked to be reported. I don't think they understood, they just wished us a good voyage. We had a finch type bird aboard for a few hours, a long way from its destination. The boom seems to be holding well and we pump a lot, 800 strokes an hour in calm conditions. I hope it won't go above that normally or we shall be strained by double watches.

Saturday night was a long one of the usual sort. Everything seemed

O.K. at dinner time, we were running smoothly at 3 knots. We decided on a double watch, and by midnight we had three rolls in. By one another three. 2.30 and off came the mainsail which takes an hour in a gale in the dark. The glass was steady all the while. It started to fall during the morning, and at breakfast time we dropped the staysail and ran under bare poles dead down wind in the exact direction we wanted to go. We tried the storm jib as we had difficulty at first keeping her from broaching. This blew out, not surprising as I think it came with the boat in 1902. By this time we had the hang of it and it was 24 hours before we put up the staysail. We did about three knots under poles. Now the barometer is steadily going up, and the wind has freshened to Force 5, so we keep the mainsail lashed down, still on double watches. She rolls like the spoilt child she is, or is it spoilt old lady? This is very tiring to start with, as it is hard work helming, but one gets used to it in time, and luckily she makes little water, that is, less water. We still have to keep pumping. We had one big sea on board which destroyed two wooden stanchions, removed some of the gunwale and the fenders — you can now see daylight over Brian's bunk, and if we are hove to or we roll under it is going to pour in. It was a good experience to run under bare poles and we have made a lot of miles out of it although we could have made more. We are now well on our way to Lymington. There will be much to do when it gets calmer, filling up a few holes and attempting the repairs.

I spoke too soon about water coming in; Ilan heard it pouring in under the galley, and I've managed to screw a piece of copper over a tingle while we were heeled over. That seems to have fixed it. An equinoctial gale has hit us and the mainsail has started to go and brought the topping lift down. Jonno has volunteered to go up in my climbing harness, good boy. Into Shannon and another gale to celebrate my 21st birthday — Ilan did us proud with moussaka and peaches in rum. What better way to celebrate this occasion. The storms continue but we have seen the Lizard light and home gets nearer. I shall have to go up once more to repair the jib block, another casualty. I shall be glad to get to the end of the voyage in many ways, but I know it has been very important to me, particularly knowing the Old Man. He was almost human this evening, unlike the time when those friends of his came on board. As they left he said, 'God, I thought they would never leave, I couldn't stand their conversation.' I know what he meant, but he put it so aggressively. He's definitely a shy man, and aggressive as many shy people get. It makes him really unpleasant at times, although he probably doesn't mean it. The other night we were talking about his crews: 'maybe I have been unlucky.' People find him intolerant, I don't think he is, he sums you up, makes an opinion, and then keeps you up to it. He knows people's limitations, can and does accept them. He then keeps you up to those limitations, he is very like Paddy Tritton in that respect. He doesn't like mistakes when you should know better, but knows he has his own limitations. These humane qualities must always have been there, but it seems that it is only the last few years that have brought them out. Everyone thinks of him as an ogre and crawls around. He would much prefer it if people stood up for themselves — really stood up. He always puts the final word in, which we shouldn't let him do. His outward behaviour is so different from what he must feel. I think he will ask me to come again, but I only hope he has some decent repairs done. When I had finished the exhaust that time and blue smoke poured out, I wasn't ashamed of my work, I just felt that I had let him down. Why should I feel so subservient to him — no, not exactly that. I knew he would feel ill of me if I made an obvious balls up, he wouldn't just say 'Oh dear, we'll have to try something else.' I don't think he can comprehend the sort of things I have done, because he's always had someone like me aboard, I suppose. He does the wire splicing, I do the engine maintenance. I don't question him, nor he me. I am sure he would love to unburden a whole lot of things on one, but he won't, or can't. Ask him if he enjoyed a book . . . 'Oh yes'. Lots of sympathy, but 'though I thought it a bit far-fetched' and that's all. He then either goes on reading or may talk briefly of something else. He doesn't ask one questions about life; he will listen, but not pry. Just the shyness, I suppose, or perhaps he values his castle — must be your own master — learn from your own experience, not others' — my philosophy except that I try to learn from others, being young. Do I have a philosophy? I feel I think more about it than I have ever begun to put on paper. At least, I hope so, reading between bits. I remember now that first day Angus and I came upon the boat. We had gone to Mylor Bridge to the yard there in the slight rain — at the bottom of the steep hill I stopped the car and we looked at her up against the quay. The strong and the weak. There was no doubt about it, I thought it was going to be tough. Small wizened old man, tough, wiry disciplinarian, but no, a sad old man, let down so he thinks by countless people — his own fault — and sometimes I feel worthless. I will always value this trip, and set other things against it, like my friendship with Ilan. This long time at sea certainly puts things into perspective. I remember thinking how the cold sharpened and cleared the mind; now we think only of the essentials. Not often can or does my mind run loose, except perhaps to think of the relief of getting to Lymington. Perhaps I should not have started on this long and distant journey. We live from one day to the next trying to forget, ignore and be patient with one another's foibles, and think only for ourselves — not of, but for ourselves. I suppose I am tired of the continuous movement added to all the travelling last year, not the duration but the sustained intensity. To travel like this one's patience must be infinite, and certainly one's in a vicious circle. If one fights against the difficulties, never disagreeing, shying off all controversial ideas one gets so pent up. These long hours we put in cures it to a great extent, there's so much to do and so little time to think, more mistakes, the possibility of short rations. It seems miles to Lymington with all its boats and trains. If anyone asked me why I should want to go to such a godforsaken part of the world I can answer that it's not only the remoteness, because being in the Atlantic provides that. It's not just the being there, the thousands of miles from London. The beauty of the ice and land, the ice in particular, and the tent homes. The scenery looks inviting in summer, not bleak and hostile at all. I can't quite describe what it is, but I know it, and I know it is where I shall want to come back to.

Dear Parents,

On the eve of what must be one of the happiest days of your life, I am only sorry that I cannot be with you to share that joy. When I left England I assumed that there would be no hope of being back as we would be about 1,000 miles from the North Pole with four people to depend on and them me. We were delayed in Cork and then in Castletown, near Bantry after damage from the North Atlantic. I still thought no more of it. When we got to Cape Farewell three weeks later and the temperature went down to almost freezing, with icebergs the size of Stockbridge looming at one out of the fog, I realised that it was the 16th of July. It looked as if it was then possible for me to get back, although I did not want to be selfish with regard to the others. I started realising how much the union of your daughter meant to you and me, and I soon hoped that perhaps we would arrive in Godthaab at exactly the right time — I looked up the planes from Stromfjord to Copenhagen, Copenhagen to London and back. I could leave S.S. at midday Friday, be in London 0230 Saturday, leave London midnight Sunday and be back in S.S. Monday midday. By this time we were making progress about 30 miles a day and I started working it out that we should arrive on Thursday. About Saturday it looked as if I would never get there at all, at which a southerly gale arose, the skies cleared, we saw the sun and we raced Godthaab-wards. Wednesday evening the storm abated 10 miles from Godthaab. The gods were obviously on our side — at which the fog descended — visibility back to normal, about 100 yards, and we edged our way into a fjord that wasn't Godthaab at all but one further up the coast. At midday the fog cleared and we motored the last 50 miles into Godthaab and dropped anchor 5.30. I hoped that there would be a helicopter connection to S.S. the next morning, so off I trundled to the Airport. Yes, there was a connection leaving at eight o'clock Friday morning — me 'Absolutely no chance of a seat? stand by?' — ' — no, no chance, never happens,' the gods had let me down. The day before all flights were cancelled so today's were chock ablock. Anyway this morning I heaved myself up at 5.30 and sat in the Airport and watched, heart falling, while 16 people arrived, checked in and walked to the waiting 'copter. I was only satisfied when it actually left the ground with maximum number of people on board. I felt £500 the richer but sad. I did my best, I thought, so my conscience is clear. I bought a bottle of the best Champagne the capital of 3,000 people can provide, some Cordon Rouge and a pound of their best caviar which we shall have at noon tomorrow.

I remember saying at the beginning of this year that I would not push for the Round the World Race but if it came up I would drop everything else and go, which I did. By April I had two definite berths on it, although one not satisfactory. I still considered that this would be the be all and end all of experience for one of my age. Ever since leaving the straight and narrow I have wanted to do something properly, something big. Then Tilman appeared on the scene with something proper, an end, something to achieve, something difficult but wholly regardless. This was to be something that I mustn't miss. I might not enjoy it — a grumpy old man who can't stand anybody — cold, wet and discomfort, but I knew I had to come and that I would regret it if I didn't. And I would have done. This will be one of the greatest things that I will do in the next few years. I now feel, after nearly three months on board, content, satisfied and really happy. These months of pleasure have been worth waiting for and I think I will look back and remember them vividly. The worry and doubt of giving up University and jumping from one thing to another are nothing. The cold does it. It is not bad now but for about week, from Cape Farewell north-west, as cold as we'll have. At night on watch in driving rain one's mind clears. You forget the small unimportant things of life which immediately puts things into proper perspective. I have kept a vast diary of events and a few ideas so I won't go into the details of the actual trip. To start off with it blew hard, then was flat calm and then foggy with about a three day cycle, and progress was hopeless. It was then foggy and overcast for a week, but we made up the miles. At Cape Farewell it was totally foggy and we had one very near miss luckily in day time. Brian shouted down that there was a berg ahead and we'd better go about — no one moved — 'You'd better hurry.' The Old Man and I were out of our bunks like scared rabbits and then proceeded to waste half a minute putting our boots on (die with our boots on) came up on deck to find a vast wall of cold ice about twenty yards away, we were just missing it. We watched in awe (numinous) not moving a muscle. We knew that if one thing went wrong we might/would spend the rest of our lives freezing to death on a piece of ice the size of Winchester Cathedral (ridge tiles and all). We were all frightened to death. Very sobering and mind clearing, like the firing squad. Anyway my standards have risen and I will never accept anything that isn't as interesting as sailing in a ropey old boat to Greenland. Ellesmere is now out, which saddens the Old Man, but we will be happy in going to visit the geologist friend in Umanak — another four hundred miles to the north, 1,200 from the pole. We should get some climbing in there. The Devil's Thumb, rather like the Old Man of Hoy but substantially bigger, has only been climbed once before, we reckon. I might be the first British man to stand on the top, I shall certainly have a go at it. Introduce the Old Man to rock climbing and drag him off — or vice versa. If we can get near enough. This is a great country. No one worries about you or stares but they are all very kind and helpful. All the Danes speak English, which is useful. The countryside is bleak, barren and snow-patched and very beautiful — a bit like Dartmoor and the Lake District. A lot of the mountains look just like Great Gable only twice the size. I have taken hundreds of photographs and have many postcards which I won't send but store up.

We leave probably on Tuesday morning for the north, where we will eat seal, whale and cod caught by me I hope — not the whale. We've seen quite a few of these — occasionally they come really close and one is frightened to death. An animal almost as long as the boat and twenty feet away is a very powerful force. They suddenly appear, which is even worse. All of a sudden behind you is a great hissing of air and rush of water — you turn round to see this black thing like a submarine appear from nowhere looking as if it might draw you and the boat down with it.

Anyway you will hear and read about it when I return probably at the end of September (with nothing to do). I will be thinking of you tomorrow and hope everything goes exactly as planned and desired.
All my love,
Simon.

BAROQUE CAME INTO Lymington on 7 October. Major Tilman had hoped to make the tide but the wind was against him, so, as the engine was out of action, he arranged a tow. Typically, he says that it was an ignominious end to a voyage but Simon's description was very different: it was Sunday and there were many other craft about, *Baroque* was festooned with weed and looked pretty battered. The crew of the first yacht that noticed their condition asked where on earth they had come from, and the reply 'The Arctic' produced a suitably gratifying reaction. By·the time the tow had been arranged and *Baroque* neared her berth, word had gone round that Tilman was home, the Island Ferry blew her sirens, people waved and cheered, and she sailed in to a hero's welcome.

Dicky and I went down to collect Simon. Major Tilman had already gone ashore, so I am sorry that they never met, but when Dicky saw the condition of *Baroque* he was glad that he hadn't seen her before Simon set off. He could stick a thumbnail into most of the timber. Simon looked and smelt so incredible that we had to apologize to the waitresses and our neighbours at dinner in the hotel and they were suitably impressed.

The dirt of the last four months had barely been soaked off when a letter arrived from Alan Cowley, whom Simon had last seen in Porto Ercole. It was from Terneuzen in Holland asking if Simon would go and help him to convert the barge *Johanna*, which he had bought when he sold the German E boat they were living on. Simon very much wanted to learn to work with steel so he packed up his tools and some more old clothes to replace the ones I'd burnt when he left *Baroque* and set off. *Johanna* was moored on a canal beside the Harvée factory where ships were being extensively repaired and redesigned, and where there was a team of ten welders led by a German foreman. I've talked to Alan about this period — though for quite a long time Alan couldn't speak of Simon without distress — and learned a lot about Simon. This is what he told me:

The first thing to be done on *Johanna* was to cover the main bulk of the barge with steel plates, and as neither of them could weld Alan thought he'd have to get a contract welder; but Simon silently and determinedly got hold of the welding plant Alan had brought and started to practice. At first it was catastrophic, holes in everything, but in a short time his weldings had strength if not beauty. When winter came he spent hours in freezing cold that Alan couldn't stand, then he taught Alan to weld and between them they put on the whole roof — 48 feet by 12 feet, curved, hundreds of square feet and Simon did 90 per cent of it. The plates were too big to lift, they had to be swung on by crane and clamped down, and while Simon welded Alan cut the ends.

Alan did most of the woodwork and Simon the electrical wiring, three phases, A.C. and single phase A.C. and 24 volt D.C., which would have cost many hundreds of pounds professionally. Simon did all the drawings and planning and it all still works well. He made all the switches out of the marine boxes taken from the E boat, and left a logbook of the circuits and fuses. Alan says that Simon had an analytical and inventive mind: he never accepted a principle because it was standard practice, but always tried to improve on it and his innovations worked. An example which Alan gave — which I don't pretend to understand — was the design of the engine controls. They both liked traditional rather than modern design, which was evident in Simon's conversion of *En Avant*, and Alan had some very attractive old brass engine controls which he wanted to use on the modern engine he'd bought for *Johanna*. Simon designed the system of control from the engine to the gearbox and throttle, and made the wheels and cogs and all the rods of stainless steel, forward and neutral and reverse. It is a joy to Alan and unique because it is positive, all by rods; all the angles had to be worked out because the levers change the angle of the rod. It had to be carefully designed, the same angle on the brackets as on the wheels, a feat of precision and still working perfectly. Alan was impressed by the tremendous enthusiasm and dedication Simon gave to any piece of work, his determination to do it well and to finish it, not for himself but for the sake of a job well done. He worked all hours, and refused any pay, but was delighted when Alan gave him the old Deutz engine from *Johanna*.

Alan recounted two incidents, both of which I feel threw light on Simon's character and confirmed my understanding. The first related to his daughter, Emma, who was at that time about eighteen months old: Alan and Simon were working on deck and Alan had to go across to the factory to collect some more welding rods. He sat Emma on a seat in the wheelhouse above the stairway and told Simon to keep an eye on her while he was away. When Alan came back he found that Emma had toppled over and fallen right down the stairs on her head, and, being frightened in case she was seriously hurt, he lost his temper and let fly at Simon. Simon made no attempt at excuses, he let Alan finish and then said how sorry he was and wished he had taken more care of her. Alan was impressed that someone so determined and single-minded was so balanced and unaggressive, though, he said, in the sort of difficult situation that sometimes arose with drunken seamen, Simon could be very tough and never opted out through fear. The other incident which Alan told me was so graphic that I shall put it in his words: 'We were both welding from a big gas bottle, and a piece of molten weld fell on the pipe and the pipe caught fire. I grabbed Simon and said "Run." Simon said "But the boat'll go up," and I said "Bugger the boat, run." There wasn't one man in the Harvée factory, not one welder, who would have gone anywhere near it, they would have run for their lives, and I would have run only Simon didn't, so I couldn't. Simon put the flame out, he turned the gas off. The flame was coming up through the tube, and when it got to the bottle it was going to explode, and Simon went up to it and turned it off with the key. You have to get the special key and put it in a slot and turn it round. It saved my boat.'

Simon came back to England in the spring of 1974 and immediately got in touch with Major Tilman, and was very pleased when he was invited to join a voyage in *Baroque* to circumnavigate Spitzbergen. They were to leave at the end of May. Simon always kept in touch with three Wykehamist friends, Angus Clarke, Christopher Lloyd Owen and Rowley Staniland, and between them they hatched a plan to borrow Angus' father's boat and sail off westward for a week or two. Simon drove my mini to collect the others and take them to Lymington where the boat lay. They sailed over to the Island and spent the night in the Newtown river, and it was there at breakfast the next morning that Simon had one of the psychic experiences that I can't call precognition because he didn't know what was going to happen. Nor was it clairvoyance. He simply knew that he had to come home, though at that time all was well; Dicky was going to his office for the last time before retiring and on the way was to drop me in Andover for a day in court — the reason for Simon's premonition hadn't happened.

Simon had these odd experiences most of his life and accepted them as commonplace. There were probably many I never knew about, but I'll give another example: it happened when Simon was about sixteen and at Winchester. A young married friend of ours was living with his wife and baby in the city and Simon used to go to their house sometimes in his free time. He always enjoyed babies and small children. They had planned a holiday in France, leaving the baby with a grandmother, and told Simon they would be away for three weeks. As they said this he knew, and told them, that they would be back in nine days. They laughed and contradicted him. On the eighth day of their visit the grandmother found the baby dead in its cot, and on the morning of the ninth day its parents were back in England. My friend the grandmother told me the news, and I spoke to Simon on the telephone to warn him not to burst into the house if he saw lights on. His reaction was almost of guilt. 'I couldn't have prevented it, I didn't know why they were coming back, I just knew they were.' I reassured him that no one could have prevented a cot death. I don't give any explanation of these happenings, I just recount them. If Simon had ever told me not to do something I had planned I would not have done it.

On this day Simon told the others to their annoyance that he must come home, and asked them to put him back to Lymington. This they did, and he drove home to find the house empty. He never bothered with a key, he climbed up and into our bedroom window to find the bedside telephone ringing. It was a call from Dicky's office to say that he had had a stroke and been taken to Winchester hospital. By the time a message had been got to me in court (I was a magistrate) and I walked into the retiring room Simon was standing there. We drove to Winchester to find that Dicky was conscious and making a joke of talking out of one side of his mouth, but he couldn't see us. Within an hour he was deeply unconscious and we were told that he was not expected to live the night. In fact he lived for ten days, looking so peacefully asleep that I felt I could wake him up to say I'd had enough of coping without him, it was time he woke and started living again. Simon and I — Selina was in Portsmouth with John — drove backwards and forwards to the hospital. When we got there we couldn't do anything so we drove home and when we got home I wanted to go back to the hospital. Every late night visit we thought would be the last, and Simon insisted that I woke him before telephoning for news first thing in the morning. I was deeply grateful for the peacefulness of Dicky's death and for Simon's wordless support. When he told me that he had written to Major Tilman explaining that he couldn't join the Spitzbergen expedition I protested that it wasn't necessary for him to stay, that there were no immediate decisions to be made, no question of moving from the house. I asked Selina to persuade him that I really meant it and would hate him to give up the opportunity out of a sense of duty. The answer that came back was quite uncompromising — he didn't want to go and that was an end to it. Major Tilman was very understanding; as it turned out that voyage was a sad one for him because his dear sister, with whom he lived in Wales, died before he reached home. He spoke to her on the telephone from his landfall in England and told her when to expect him back, but by the time he landed in Lymington she had suddenly and unexpectedly died. He wrote to Simon, 'Death clouded the beginning and end of the voyage.'

Simon felt that his father's death, which affected him deeply, meant that he should get a job in England and settle down for a bit. He was very lucky to get one in Scotland, for which Iain Clarke, Angus' father, recommended him. It was at the new port, Portavadie, on Loch Fyne, where Sea Platforms, a consortium, were building a harbour and plant under a government scheme for producing oil rigs. Simon was to live in the hotel at Kames with three engineers. He was offered a good wage, a long weekend off in four, and all expenses paid. It was absolutely up Simon's street, hard work against the clock, creating something. He was able to save practically all his salary, because there was nothing there to spend it on but beer and he didn't drink much of that. He was there from April to the end of October, by which time the port was built but no orders for any oil rigs had materialized so the plant had to be run down.

The other engineers, all qualified, were older men, I think, and Simon told me that when there was a problem to be solved his suggestions would be laughed at as not being by the book; but very often the next day one of them would get him alone and ask to hear them again, and sometimes they would prove to be the only solution. I know Simon enjoyed the work very much, and I think he did well because this is what one of his superiors has said of him:

Simon was appointed in April 1975 as Assistant Marine Controller on the basis of a good academic record and greater than average knowledge of boats, ships, the sea and those who sail on it. The post required energy, zeal, versatility, diplomacy and intelligence. He had all these qualities and more besides. He proved that aided by his good technical general knowledge he was able to direct his brain to designing jetty facilities, Ro/Ro ramps etc., and what is even more important to get them built whilst doing other things simultaneously. He was readily able to assimilate technical requirements and his keen enquiring mind was always producing new ideas. He was well liked, respected, and sadly missed.

As far as I can remember, Simon came home once a month, either by air to Heathrow or tearing down the M6 in my old mini. In September on his last leave he went to Fochabers where Paddy Tritton had some fishing on the Spey. Paddy lent Simon a salmon rod; on the first three days there were no fish about, but on the last day, when Simon was due to leave after lunch, he took six good fish, a total of 58 pounds, a house record that year. According to the fishing book it was 24 September, his twenty-third birthday.

By late October the work was coming to an end. There was no prospect of any orders for oil rigs and some of the labourers had been given notice. On the morning of 22 October, Simon told me, he woke up knowing that he would leave Portavadie that day. He didn't know why, and assumed something would happen to make them pack up at once, or that he would be sacked. What did happen was quite different and unexpected, and it took him the first step on the way to realizing the venture he had begun to work out on the night watches in *Baroque*, the plan to have his own boat and take her to Smith Island in the Antarctic.

It was about nine o'clock in the morning. Ballast was being unloaded at the port from the sea. A crane with a grab was swinging it up and into waiting lorries, and Simon was supervising, particularly making sure that the new wall wasn't damaged. For some reason the back-acter of the crane swung unexpectedly and caught Simon on the bottom, scooping him up and over the wall. He fell on to the steel deck below, which, as it was low tide, was seventeen feet down. The full force of the impact, against a coaming, was taken by his right leg, shattering it just above the ankle. He told me that he remembered lying on the deck and seeing a row of horrified faces peering down at him, probably thinking he was dead. His fear was for his leg, that they might try to move him. He was aware of men on the deck beside him, and summoned all his strength to say 'Don't touch me', and then the crane driver was beside him, taking charge, sending for the first aid team and the converted Land Rover ambulance. Simon said 'This man held my hand and stroked my forehead until they came, and I couldn't've stood the pain without him.' How they got him up to the quay I don't know, I think he lost consciousness, but he did remember being in the Land Rover, and, seeing the anxiety of his friends, he managed to smile and wave as he was driven off. This gesture made an impression, because when I telephoned in response to a telegram I was told he wasn't badly hurt because he went off smiling. I was given the telephone number of the Royal Alexandra Hospital in Greenock to which he had been taken, and when I telephoned the hospital later, after he had reached the ward, I spoke to a kind practical Scots sister who told me that his broken ankle had been set and that he would be kept sedated for some time, so we agreed that I should fly up, not the next day but the one after, the 24th. The next morning at about ten o'clock, my telephone rang and the familiar voice said 'Good morning'. It was a weak voice and it rambled a bit and sometimes died away, but it was unmistakable. He complained that when he had asked for the telephone he was told that it was broken, so he demanded the pieces and screwed it all together dialled and got through. I imagined that in no time at all he would be mending all the broken bits and pieces round the hospital and hoped he wouldn't fall foul of the unions. The call lasted a long time, what with the pauses and the repetitions, and it was interesting that he was using quite uncharacter-istic phrases like 'I thought my chips were down' which he fiercely denied when I saw him the next day. The worst part he said had been the long wait alone in casualty for the effects of the morphia he had been given on site to wear off before he could have a general anaesthetic. It was a vague and disjointed conversation but neither of us wanted to end it.

The next morning I left home early to take the first shuttle from Heathrow to Glasgow and arrived at Greenock about eleven-thirty. The hospital was a gaunt forbidding building in an unsalubrious area, and my heart sank when I got to the high-ceilinged Victorian ward and found Simon among the mainly geriatric male surgical patients. The sister was delightful, she was known as Sister Olley because her Polish husband had an unpronounceable name, and she became a great ally. She told me that Doctor Ghosh (spelt GHOSH she said, pronounced as if one was saying O Gosh! which in her soft Scots accent was suitably un-English) would like to see me, and when he came he told me that the accident had caused a serious injury, but that he had decided he could save the leg. I asked him if he had to pin it, but he said no, he had set it and put it in plaster. When I expressed surprise that that was enough for a bad break he seemed to be cross and left abruptly. Sister Olley told me that they intended to keep Simon for about a month and then send him to a convalescent home, and I didn't say anything, thinking I would talk to Michael Johnson about it when I got home. I stayed until it was time to leave for the last shuttle flight. It was the first time I had seen either of my children in real pain. Simon was having injections every four hours, and the effect seemed to last about two. The referred pain from the crushed nerves convinced him that his pelvis was broken; he had been horrified during the night to find himself screaming in a ward full of sleeping men. He told me about the journey by Land Rover, about fifty rough miles through narrow roads, the ferry being held up for him, then the long wait alone in casualty. In a cowardly way I was relieved when the time came to leave. Next day I spoke to Michael and he reassured me that the hospital had an Orthopaedic department, which meant there would be a consultant surgeon, and that if the leg had not been pinned the break could not be serious. Perhaps I had misunderstood the reference to saving the leg.

Every evening I spoke to Sister Olley, and sent messages to Simon, and about a week later she said 'Mrs Richardson, could you have your boy at home?' No one had called Simon 'Your boy' for years, but I was delighted at the thought of having him at home though very surprised when she next said 'He *needs* to be at home.' We agreed that she should arrange it through the Red Cross. The next evening, a Friday, my telephone rang and Sister Olley's voice said 'Good news, Mrs Richardson, your boy'll be at Heathrow in an hour.' This was a bit of a shock, because we are about sixty miles from Heathrow and I only had a mini, but I rang Eric Fenning at the garage — woe be to he who has no friends — and within minutes we were speeding up the M3 in his big Wolseley, leaving two friends who happened to be staying to get a bed downstairs into the dining room. The plane had landed when we arrived, and it was a nightmare trying to find Simon in the confusion of the Friday evening rush of the domestic flight terminal. As I was hurrying through the crowd to where I remembered the Glasgow shuttle landed, a stranger walking towards me stopped, came back and said 'Are you Mrs Richardson? I've got your son here.' I was amazed that he had picked me out of the crowd, and even more so when he said it was because of my likeness to Simon. Simon was in a wheelchair looking awful and he must have been relieved to see us. He had planned, if I was not there, to go by tube to

Waterloo with the man he'd come down with, a Sea Platforms employee, and from there get a train to Winchester. What had happened at the other end was this: Sister Olley had got in touch with the Red Cross, but had been told that time would be needed to organize the transfer home as an ambulance from Heathrow to Hampshire would have to cross two county boundaries. Also the air line would require Simon to take three seats to put his leg up, and preferably to be accompanied by a nurse. Very expensive, so Simon decided not to wait for all that — for one thing he wasn't eating any of the hospital food which didn't surprise me, having been offered lunch the day I went up — and instead asked his friends at Sea Platforms to help. Two colleagues who were travelling to London for the weekend arrived at the hospital with a van. The lift was out of order, but, using the two sticks lent to him, Simon got himself down two flights of stairs and they heaved him into the back of the van which arrived at the airport just as the shuttle was about to leave. Simon was determined to get himself on to it and started hobbling along the tarmac, at which the pilot, who was standing at the top of the boarding ramp, saw him and called out to him not to hurry but to take his time, and that the plane would not leave without him. Simon hauled himself aboard by the strength in his arms, and found that another passenger had been asked to move along and a beer crate had been brought to the gangway to make a leg rest for the hour-long flight. The pilot then radioed ahead and arranged for a wheelchair and an attendant to meet the plane, and on arrival Simon was swung out with the luggage.

Over the next few days I heard from Simon the story of his stay in the Royal Alexandra Hospital in Greenock, and I must say that if subsequent events had not confirmed it I should have wondered if he had dreamt it all. Two days after the accident he was seen by the consultant surgeon, who examined the X-rays and decided that the fragmented bones were not in alignment. He had the plaster cut all round the ankle for a width of about an inch, gave Simon an injection of Valium, and, with a mallet, drove wooden wedges down between the ankle and the plaster to alter the angle. Simon passed out. The next day, a walking iron having been put under the foot, a physiotherapist, 'about half my size' came and said she was going to get him out of bed to walk. As he stepped on the leg they both crashed to the ground, Simon unconscious. The next day the same thing happened with a slightly larger physiotherapist, and it was then I think that Sister Olley thought he might be better at home.

Once home and comfortably installed in the dining room Simon perked up quite well though he still watched the clock for when the next pain killer would be due. Michael came the next day and when he saw the walking iron on Simon's plaster he reassured us that it couldn't be a serious break. An appointment was made for Simon to see the orthopaedic surgeon, Kenneth Hesketh, in Winchester Hospital at his next clinic, Friday 7 November. By the time we drove in on that day the pain had subsided to bearable limits, and Simon expected to be told that the bones were mending well and given a routine future appointment. I went with him only because he was unable to drive, not for support; so the shock when it came was unexpected. We were called to Mr Hesketh's room where the X-ray of Simon's leg was on the wall. Kenneth Hesketh, a man of few words, told Simon that the damage to his leg was considerable, that the bones were fragmented and unless they were pinned there was no possibility that he would ever walk again. Simon looked as if it were a physical blow. He'd had sixteen days of agonizing but decreasing pain, and the thought that it was all going to start again was too much to bear. He said quite aggressively that no one was going to touch his leg, and he'd no reason to believe that this different opinion was the right one. Kenneth Hesketh was kindly brutal and said 'You haven't got a leg. If this isn't done you won't ever walk again.' I agreed that it must be done and that as we had a B.U.P.A. subscription, and our experience of National Health hadn't been reassuring, we would like it to be done privately. Kenneth very fairly said that even on the National Health there was no question of one of his staff doing the operation, he was the Consultant, but Simon would have to wait longer. As the waiting was not going to be easy we thought it should be done in the private wing, and arrangements were made for Simon to go in the following Tuesday, 11 November, for an operation the next day. That weekend put a great strain on Simon, and I didn't find it very easy. A young artist friend, Julia Whatley, did a watercolour portrait of him during that time which exactly catches the haunted look, the memory of pain and the fear of more to come.

On the evening of the 11th Simon went into Ashley ward of the County Hospital and the plaster was cut off his leg. It was a horribly bruised and deformed object which emerged, swollen and monstrous, more like a club foot than a normal one, with two deep infected wounds; when I went the next day after Kenneth's entirely successful operation it was a great relief to see an elegantly plastered leg exactly

Claude Richardson

Dorothy Richardson with Selina and Simon (1954)

Simon aged 2

Simon aged 4

Simon aged 8

Simon aged 13

Above: Simon aged 20, on board *Baroque*

Right: On Mount Change, Greenland

Above: Simon aged 22, with Mark Johnson

Below: Simon in bed after the accident negotiating on the telephone for *En Avant*

Above: 2 days before the accident: Paddy Tritton and Simon preparing to go fishin on the Spey

Below: Simon convalescing

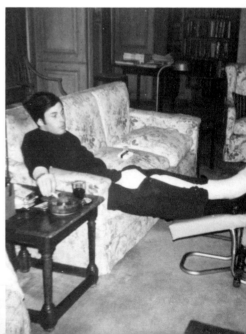

En Avant as she
was when
bought

En Avant, with her
superstructure
removed, arriving
in Southampton
Water

En Avant in
Smith's
boatyard,
Southampton

Above left: Mark Johnson and H. W. Tilman taking sun sights on the way to Rio

Above: Heavy seas on the way to Rio

Left: Simon in the Doldrums, wearing the Robinson Crusoe hat he made out of an old sail

Below: Simon's 25th birthday party, September 24th 1977

the same as the good one but a little thicker. Simon must have been an interesting patient; he wouldn't eat in hospital, although the food in Winchester was really very good, but he drank enormous quantities of water, in order I think to have the nurses coming in often to empty his bottle. He wouldn't wear anything at all in bed, nor have anything but a sheet over him, and a little modesty towel was kept by the bed to cover his manliness when the sheet was removed. He insisted on having the window of his room wide open at the bottom, so the poor girls had to wear their cloaks to go in and nurse him. Kenneth had said that he would not be able to go home until he could manage stairs: on Sunday the 16th he decided that the time had come and demanded a stick to try the stairs. To Sister's surprise and probably her relief he managed to get up and down the next flight and came home.

Kenneth Hesketh to Michael Johnson 18.11.1975.

I admitted Simon Richardson on the 11th and the following day under general anaesthesia explored his ankle.

The medial malleolus was found detached with a flap of inturned periosteum and soft tissue, which was removed and the malleolus was screwed into place. I then explored the lower quarter of the tibia which was comminuted and impacted in less than ideal position. It has been possible to disimpact the fracture and reduce the fragment into good position with multiple screw fixation and a small loose fragment of the anterior tibial margin of the ankle joint has been fixed in place with a Kirschner wire.

The next period, when Simon was at home but more or less immobilized, was great fun. He held court in his bed in the dining room and many of his friends came to see him, and we laughed a lot. Unfortunately Mark was on one of his long voyages so he couldn't come, but many others did. One trick which Simon learned and which gave him a lot of quiet fun was to use his bottle unobtrusively without withdrawing from the conversation, which he said is not as easy as it sounds. Once he saw a cock pheasant in the garden and demanded that I brought Dicky's gun and some cartridges, and he loaded up and got me to support him hopping outside to stalk the wretched bird, until my imagination of the possible headlines in the local paper got the upper hand and I mutinied. There was a total eclipse of the moon due during this period, and Simon hopped into the drawing room where I opened the big sliding bay window over the river and pulled the sofa up for him. It was a glorious clear cold starry night and we both wrapped ourselves in duvets and sat without speaking through the whole majestic movement.

Simon decided to use the time while he was out of action in learning three things: to play the piano, type, and cut lettering. He borrowed Mark's first books of theory, made me search out the Pitman's typing course, and wrote to our good friends Will and Barbara Carter of the Rampant Lions Press in Cambridge for advice. They came down to see him and Will brought a piece of lime wood and a little cutting tool, and Simon cut his name quite passably, SIMON, which I have as a reminder of a very happy time. The other two good intentions never got off the ground because as soon as he had recovered his equilibrium after the operation his whole attention was turned to the next and most exciting development of his life, the expedition to Smith Island which had been germinating since the nights on watch in the Arctic. He had had a letter from Major Tilman on November the 17th.

Dear Simon,

It was nice to hear from you, even as a cripple. It sounds like a really nasty mishap. You don't say whether you are now mobile or on crutches or what.

This year's cruise proved a bit disappointing. We started too late anyway to make Ellesmere Is. but I thought at least Upernaish or a bit further. However on August 7th off the south corner of Disko Is. the boom broke clean in two. It had only just been hoisted when it happened. There was no hope of splinting or scarphing as there were two separate pieces. So I gave up in disgust, called at Holsteinborg for bread and water, and came home direct. A fast passage, too, without the mainsail, with a fine quartering wind of 5 or 6 nearly all the way. On the way out we got too near C. Farewell and had some ice trouble, a day wasted and two planks opening. The Berthon are making a solid boom but I now wish I had asked for an extra inch diameter. Crew on the whole very good except for one for whom I conceived a quite vicious hate. I had great trouble finding them, touch and go right up to the last minute.

You may remember my friend, Professor Drever at Igdlorssuit, a geologist from St Andrews. He died of a heart attack less than a month ago. Two other old friends who went about the same time were John Tew, the surveyor. He was the manager at the Berthon when I first had *Mischief* there. The other was little Tom Northern who used to visit the boat at Lymington, wheel-driver in my battery in France in 1916.

I am hoping to go north next year, probably (almost certainly) the last time. So far I have had two offers but one is in America.

I am in Southampton for a lecture for the R.S.Y.C. on Thursday, December 11th and hope to visit Lymington just to look at the boat on the Friday before returning to London for a train back here. I'm all alone here now and except for a long sea voyage, when arrangements can be made, it is difficult to be away much.

Sandy Lee, I'm glad to say, is going strong and a great help for me now that Putto is gone.

Yours ever,

H. W. Tilman.

Simon must have seen this proposed journey south as an opportunity to discuss the Smith Island plan, and I was asked to write and invite Major Tilman to stay. I don't know if Simon had already met Pam Davis, Major Tilman's niece, who lived with her husband Derek at Herriard near Alton, or why he thought it might be useful to try out on her the idea of inviting her uncle to join him; but he telephoned to her and we were both invited, I as chauffeur, to go over on the morning of 3 December. Simon outlined his plan, and when he got to the part about asking H. W. Tilman, Bill Tilman the world-famous climber and sailor, to crew for him Pam was amazed and almost speechless. 'You dare not ask Bill Tilman to sail with you,' she said. 'He can refuse,' said Simon. 'He'll make mincemeat of you,' was her reaction, and indeed mine too. When Major Tilman came to stay later that month I don't know if Simon made the offer or what passed between them. Major Tilman must have been planning his '76 voyage in *Baroque*, and Simon knew there was no possibility of going before '77, so there was plenty of time. He hadn't even got a boat yet, though he had his earnings from Sea Platforms saved up so he could think of buying one. He knew exactly what he wanted, a steel ship that would not break up in icy waters, and small enough to get in close to the sheer cliffs of Smith Island. He had been much attracted to the salvage tugs that worked in and out of Terneuzen in Holland when he was working there with Alan Cowley, and he telegraphed to ask him if any were for sale. There was one that had been involved in an accident while pulling something that proved too heavy for her: she had run in under the larger vessel and sank, killing one of her crew. The superstructure had been irretrievably damaged and she was for sale. The asking price was £2,500, but Alan eventually made a deal on Simon's behalf for £750. In Simon's writing case, along with his journal, I later found a note in his handwriting:

I Bought a Tug — Life on a luxury yacht — '77 Admirals Cup Contender
   It took me the best part of six months to buy *En Avant XV*. I had known all along that I wanted the boat and I at last bought her on February 3rd, for £750 — now she is called *ex En Avant*.

I presume this means that he had seen her, or one of her sister ships, when he was first in Terneuzen and had worked from April to October saving up to buy her. He referred to her as 'ex En Avant' because one of the conditions of the sale was that her name should be changed; *En Avant* was the name of all the chain of tugs owned by the Mullers in Terneuzen, *En Avant* and then a serial number. Simon thought of various other names for her, and I think his favourite was 'The Quest', after Shackleton's ship. Originally we thought of her as 'The Quest', but gradually this condition seemed to lapse, perhaps because the Mullers were interested in Simon's plan and were happy to have the name associated with it. They wrote to him later asking if they could have a photograph of her, with sails set, for their Christmas calendar, and he said he would be glad to provide one for a fee of £750.
   Immediately the sale was agreed Simon went out to Holland. It was fourteen weeks since his accident, he was still in a cumbersome thigh-length plaster, walking with two sticks, and it was February. I was to drive him to Dover, and we planned to leave at first light, but the forecast on the evening B.B.C. News was of snow spreading from the north-east, and the A.A. appealed to motorists not to drive. Simon decided to catch a train at once for Waterloo, spend the night with a friend in Richmond and go on to Dover by train the next day. He put his rucksack on the roofrack of the mini and packed it there with all his tools, including his big Bosch steel-cutter. By the time it was full the rucksack must have weighed about a hundredweight, and when we got to Winchester station we had difficulty in getting it on to his back. I had parked at the back entrance to save walking down and under the line, but it meant two flights of stairs up. Simon had his sticks and I went behind him trying to support a little of the weight of his burden, but I really feared he wouldn't be able to manage the second flight, or

that the plaster would crack. However he got to the top, telling me that the more weight one put on a broken bone the quicker it fused together. At that time there were reports of several incidents on the London Underground late at night, gangs of youths attacking and robbing travellers, and I knew that Simon had £1,000 in notes in his rucksack; however no one in their senses would have suspected it from his appearance, nor perhaps have risked being within range of his sticks. But I had a pang when the train pulled out.

Alan met him in Zeebrugge, and said he was in considerable pain and the weight he was carrying had made his leg swell and they could see he had lost a lot of weight. He lived aboard *Johanna* with the Cowleys, he and Alan each working on their own boat but helping the other when necessary, Simon's plaster getting more and more bashed and covered with oil and dirt. Periodically he came back to see the surgeon, and it was a great relief to him when it finally came off. This was sometime in June, I think, and he arranged on the same visit to take back the Deutz engine which Alan had previously given him, and which was sitting in an outhouse here in pieces. It weighed three tons, it was a two cylinder Deutz diesel air-start engine with two air bottles, one to start her, one in reserve.

Simon had persuaded his godfather, William Walford, who farmed in Somerset, to help with his Land Rover and trailer, and at 8.30 on the morning after the plaster came off we started to load. Simon rigged up a pair of sheerlegs and a pulley, using the crutches which he had been given at the hospital to avoid putting too much weight on his leg to hitch the pulley-rope over the sheerlegs. With various friends helping we got the whole collection of rusty-looking bits safely stowed, and William and Simon started for Dover, the crutches prominently lashed on top to distract the customs officials. Alan thought Simon would find it impossible to get the engine working again, that he would need a skilled engineer. The belt was loose, and they had had great difficulty getting the flywheel off. It was a pity Simon didn't know he was going to buy a boat in Terneuzen, a lot of trouble would have been saved, however Simon reassembled it, and got Mr Dreece the Terneuzen expert to check the alignment of the prop, and the engine generally. The valve timing was slightly out, but otherwise Mr Dreece was satisfied with it, and I think it was the only possession Simon really cared about.

In August the Cowleys were ready to leave Terneuzen and take *Johanna* down through the French canals to Le Somail on the Canal du Midi where she still is. Simon was not yet able to leave; though the engine was reassembled he had not yet had it running, nor had he found any of his friends able to help him bring the boat back to England. I don't quite know how it happened, and I don't remember any of the relevant conversation, I just know that during his first visit home after the Cowleys left I found myself offering to go back to Terneuzen with Simon. We loaded various necessary pieces of equipment, pots and pans, a Belling grill-boiler, plastic buckets and as much food as possible (because of the poor Dutch exchange rate) into the back of a little Saab van which Eric Fenning sold Simon for £300, and set off for Dover. It was after we'd crossed the Channel and were nearing Terneuzen that Simon said cautiously, 'I don't know what you'll think of the conditions on board, it isn't very comfortable.' 'That's all right,' I said 'I'm not expecting anything grand.' 'But,' even more cautiously, 'there's only a bucket.' 'Well, all right, I've managed with a bucket before.' 'But it's a rusty bucket.' Thank goodness we had two new plastic buckets in the van.

When we arrived at *En Avant* at dusk, I would have quailed slightly if I hadn't been with Simon. My new quarters looked like a floating scrapyard, moored on an oily-looking canal beside a steel works. The deck was a jumble of twisted metal and steel hawsers overlaid with inches of rusty iron filings. We climbed down a filthy iron ladder into the open engine-room, round a catwalk, ducked through a dwarf-sized doorway and into a dark little hole with a bunk on either side of a coffin-shaped water tank. No sign of domesticity at all. While Simon unpacked the van I picked my way among the heaps of junk on deck and found a small rusty iron table and several pieces of dirty white formica. One served to cover the table and another the tank, and when Simon had filled and lit the Tilley lamp and primus stove we had brought, I could wash the formica and instal some cooking and eating arrangements. I cooked a good meal and we opened a bottle and the cabin became very snug. There was an extraordinary overstuffed red and white flock-filled mattress from *Johanna* which Simon slept on and I had the green rexine bench seat from the back of the Saab and my sleeping bag. We had made a tiny oasis in the desert of rusty iron.

I really enjoyed the month I was there. My main function was to provide food, but I also had other jobs allotted. The first was to sort the chaos on deck, heaving useful looking bits into piles and getting Simon to remove the rubbish. Then I swept the deck and *En Avant* began to look like a boat. After that I had to clean all the small bits and pieces — the 'doofers' that might one day do for something useful —

which Simon had collected in five-gallon drums. They were standing in filthy water and I had to fish them out and scrub them with a wire brush in near-boiling water and Teepol. I started off thinking I could do this in rubber gloves but the oil and Teepol dissolved them so I stopped worrying about my hands. Water for washing I dipped out of the canal and Simon brought drinking water from the washroom at the steelworks, Harvée, which he could use, so in some ways he was luckier than me.

He was working hard on the engine. The generator was already installed, and while he had it running and the noise in the cabin was deafening I could use the Belling, but when he switched it off there was just the hiss of the Tilley and the primus. As soon as the engine was working properly we were to leave for England, a voyage which he thought would take about 36 hours. *En Avant* was to be converted to tiller steering, and this must have been done before I got there; I thought it was quite complimentary of Simon to think that I was capable of taking the helm in the North Sea at that time of the year. We were getting well into September and the equinoctial gales couldn't be far off. I was virtually in purdah and getting dirtier and dirtier. Simon spent the days working in the engine-room and driving about organizing deliveries of paraffin, diesel oil, and petrol, sometimes working quite late with the generator running. He was impervious to noise, dirt and discomfort, but I noticed that he always put his injured leg up on the bunk when he sat to eat and I think it was very much swollen by bedtime.

The food we had brought lasted very well, and I used to walk to a little corner shop on the outskirts of the town for bread and milk where my bargee-like appearance wasn't too noticeable. Once I took the car to an enormous hypermarket to stock up, which was all right until I had to hold out my hand for change at the checkout, very shaming.

Simon finished his work on the engine. It was assembled and bolted to the deck on specially cut blocks of stainless steel. Alan Cowley has described how it had a compressed air start, and he says he remembers the bottles being filled; but they certainly weren't filled when I was there. The engine had to be started without air and Simon planned to use a little five horse-power electric motor, that William Walford had given him for the purpose, powered by the Lister generator. My job was to stand by the Lister and switch it on and off as necessary. Simon meanwhile had a short steel rod inserted into the flywheel which with enormous effort he turned as I switched on the motor. I was told to watch both the motor and the generator. Black smoke from the former I could disregard, but if any came from the generator I must switch off at once. Also he told me that if the engine started the drive belt might fly off, as it was loose, so I was to go immediately behind the bulkhead, which I had no intention of doing but didn't argue.

Our getting back to England, the first step of his expedition, depended on starting the Deutz, so it was a great moment. Twice I switched on, Simon got the flywheel moving, smoke came from the motor but then from the generator so I switched off. On the third attempt Simon must have made a superhuman effort, the wheel moved faster, and suddenly the Deutz gave a great roar and came to life. Most exciting. We made a cup of tea and watched the needle of the gauge on the compression bottle climbing slowly. However our satisfaction didn't last long because Simon found the bearings in the gearbox starting to run hot and he had to stop the engine; but at least we knew there was enough air to start her again. I don't know if my description of these events makes sense technically, I may be talking nonsense, but I am writing what I remember seeing and being told.

The heating gearbox meant trouble and was a disappointment for Simon because he hoped to leave Terneuzen perhaps on the next tide, which was now out of the question. Simon didn't say anything but he sat for a long time beside the gearbox thinking, which seemed to show the benefit of a good classical education. I didn't speak to him, but at intervals I put mugs of coffee beside him. After a long while he got up and went out to talk, as I learnt later, to Mr Dreece, the engineer who had checked the alignment of the shaft earlier on. He came back with an instrument which he told me was a Vernier clock gauge which showed what he feared, that there was wear in the gearbox which put the shaft a sixteenth of an inch out of alignment. By the time this reached the engine it would perhaps have magnified to an inch. This meant he would have to undo all his work of bolting the engine down, order new blocks and move the Deutz, all three tons of it, a fraction of an inch. If it was not possible to move it he might have to dismantle it. It was not the time to speak at all, so instead I had particularly delicious food and drink ready whenever required.

As usual when there was anything difficult or unpleasant to be done Simon set to work immediately drilling out the bolts. This involved lying flat and working under the engine. It was terribly hot at the time and *En Avant* was an oven without ventilation. Sweat ran down into his eyes and misted up his protective goggles, so he took them off with the inevitable result. That evening his eyes were bright red and he seemed in trouble and admitted he'd got some steel filings in them. I think he was quite glad when I said firmly that if they were not better in the morning we would go to the hospital. Next day he could hardly open one eye. It was out of the question to go near a doctor in the state he was in, so we heated water and I washed his hair which felt like steel wool. He did his best for his face and hands, but even so he presented a pair of bloodshot eyes and gleaming white teeth in a pretty black face when we set off. It was Sunday, and the casualty department sent us to the local duty doctor; this meeting with Dr Jo Stevens, who was on that day, proved to be a blessing in disguise which relieved me of the task of helping to bring *En Avant* back to England. I just stayed until they were ready to leave and then came home on the ferry.

Simon managed to move the Deutz by the simple method of putting a crowbar under it and levering it by brute force. He had new blocks cut, and bolted it down again and restarted it. This time all ran smoothly, thank goodness, but he wasn't quite happy with the adjustment and thought another valve might have to be ground.

Alan had spoken of Cornelius Leunis, the man from whom *Johanna* had been bought, and of his affection for the Deutz; Simon looked him up in the telephone directory, and this dear little elderly man bicycled in from the village to which he had retired to help Simon tune the engine. I stayed in the cabin, hearing from the engine-room the happy sounds of two men tinkering with their toy, patting, stroking and oiling it, twisting and adjusting knobs and screws. At one time Mr Leunis demonstrated the noises it should and should not make. Their common language was the needs of the engine. Simon came through to ask me what I thought he could offer as thanks for the kindness, and suggested a bottle of whisky which seemed acceptable; but then I remembered that the teak nameboard from *Johanna*, beautifully painted and varnished, was lying where Alan had abandoned it. The last we saw of Mr Leunis was the six-foot board wobbling off on his bicycle. The Deutz was running beautifully, and soon after Simon drove me to Zeebrugge. I was sad that our life in Terneuzen had come to an end. The next time I went back was in the summer of 1983 when I sought out Jo Stevens and asked him what he remembered of Simon and their voyage in 1976. This is what he told me:

I first saw Simon on a Sunday morning when I had Dienst, as we call it here. Dienst is On Call, On Duty, and what happened on that Sunday was an interesting piece of Dienst, you might say it's what keeps me going. I saw this fellow at my door, absolutely filthy, and he had a small piece of metal, probably about half a millimetre, on his cornea. It's usually caused by grinding or welding; I tried to scrape it off, and I started to make conversation to distract him. 'How did you get this, grinding or welding?' and he said, 'Grinding'. I asked who he was working for, and he said on his own boat, *En Avant* that he'd bought from Muller. I asked him what he was going to do with her, and when he told me, 'Take her to the Antarctic', I thought of H. W. Tilman, because I had read a book of H. W. Tilman about the Antarctic called *Ice with Everything*, and when I said that, he said Well, he was Simon Richardson who was in that book. The next day he still had a lot of pain in his eye, so I sent him to the eye doctor who drilled the piece of steel out of his cornea.

When I first saw Simon I could see there was something different about him, you couldn't place him straight away. He didn't look like a Dutch workman, they are mostly a bit cleaner and they have a duller look about them; so you get a combination of a far too filthy individual with a far too sharp way of looking out of his eyes. He was unusual, that's why I started asking him questions. So we made the link about Tilman quite quickly, and then I dropped in for a cup of coffee from time to time while he was working on his boat, and it must have been the end of October when we started planning how to get her across to England. We had quite a lot of bad weather in that week, with several large vessels going down, and I remember losing some sleep because the tug had the superstructure razed off and a loose piece of plating put on top of the hole. There were some small coamings, about ten inches high, but evidently it wasn't a very seaworthy proposition; if we were going to get a lot of green water on board we'd've gone down pretty quickly, and I came to the conclusion that I should take along an inflatable life-raft.

We left at the beginning of November, the day after a heavy autumn gale, so I expected a good swell outside, also perhaps some trouble from the river police. As it was they made no trouble when we left because the visibility wasn't good and they preferred to stay inside. We left at six in the morning, it was pretty nippy and you could see no more than three to four hundred yards, you couldn't see one buoy before you lost the one you'd just passed. We managed to find the new passageway into the small fairway that goes along the Flemish coast, along the south side of the Schelde Estuary. You don't have any shipping there, and as soon as you've found your way out of the main fairway you can work your way along the coast. My job was sitting on the helmstock, that is the tiller, which was a piece of pipe about three inches in diameter, a bit cold in November but otherwise quite comfortable. The engine proved to be a joy. Sailing is one thing, but mostly the engine gives off a racket, but this one was very restful, it just gave out a couple of puffs from time to time. Simon's part of the venture was walking round the deck and making coffee and seeing the engine worked properly. In this fashion we made good time, we did seven knots on average to Dover. We went along quite close to the Belgian coast all the time and the sea was quite calm and a breeze of about Force 3, and southerly, which gave us a lee on the Belgian coast. Off the Zeebrugge mole we had an inkling of trouble because she started to roll her gunwales under two or three times in the swell that comes off the mole. After that it was plain sailing again, and we gradually worked a bit out to sea in order to get round a couple of sandbanks that lie to the south-west of Ostend.

Between Ostend and Dunkirk you have to leave the coast about three sea miles, you gradually lose sight of the coast, at least we did in that visibility. Then you have to pick up a buoy in order to be able to work your way inside the Flemish Banks. If you don't get one of those buoys, I believe there are two or three of them in the space of ten square miles, you're in trouble. We had to pick one of them up and then work our way into the coast. Just as you feel you are going to hit the beach you turn back along the coast and then you pass Dunkirk. It's an interesting piece of navigation if you haven't radar and visibility isn't good. It would have been very dark by then, and it went off quite well. It got dark as we turned into the fairway of Calais an hour later, and we had no lights, none at all, which appealed to me. The problem was the lights worked off the generator and we'd come to enjoy the peace and quiet by then, so we didn't want the generator. Simon made a good dinner of fried chicken and tomatoes and made it look like a luxury cruise — we had to use the generator for that. So there was the frozen bottom and the hot chicken in my mouth, a pleasant trip. It was a magnificent night, it was pitch dark by then and starry but no moon. Visibility was better by then, for instance off Calais we could see a loom in the air which proved to be a row of lampposts on the top of the cliffs at Dover, that must be more than twenty miles. Stars by the thousand, and lighthouses and lights around; we had a close shave with a marker buoy in the Calais fairway. They have a large dredger there that they use for getting up old wrecks, quite a large vessel, and it's marked off by four markers about 400 yards apart, and as we looked at the vessel one of the markers shot by about two yards from the boat, and shortly after we just missed a yacht, so after that we kept the generator running and the navigation lights on. The wind had freshened a bit by the time we reached Dover at about two or three in the morning. About three miles out the wind had gotten up so much we couldn't keep our course, we had to head more in the direction of North Foreland, and we got it green over the bows from time to time. The tanks that were lying around on the deck started moving around a bit. We did a couple of zigzags and weaved our way into Dover Harbour just behind one of the British Rail Ferries.

The work on *En Avant* which occupied Simon from February to October in Holland, was basically stripping her down to the hull, repairing any damage and installing an engine and generator. When he brought her back to England the conversion began. *En Avant* was 63.75ft overall, breadth 15.15ft, depth 4.9ft. She was built in Rotterdam in 1942 by Dutch slave labour for the German War effort and because she was to work in the Baltic the hull was strengthened below the water line with sixteen millimetre steel. Simon redesigned her as a gaff-rigged cutter, with accommodation for a crew of eight. The obvious port to do the work of conversion in was Southampton, only seventeen miles from home, and he arranged with a colourful character, 'Smithy' of the Belsize Boatyard on the tidal waters of the Itchen, to berth her there for £10.00 per week. She was brought there in very rough weather from Dover, and the first time I saw her again she looked exactly like all the other hulks waiting to be cut up for scrap.

The yard opened at seven every morning, and I woke Simon at a quarter to six and cooked an enormous breakfast while he dressed. He was gone by a quarter past and was home about an hour after dusk, his days lengthening with the daylight. The evenings were spent writing letters and telephoning, or watching absolute rubbish on the television which he found a complete relaxation. His leg still swelled by the end of the day, and he didn't complain when I picked it up and slid a stool under it. On 23 November he went into Sarum Road Hospital where Kenneth Hesketh took five titanium screws, one-and-a-half to one-and-three-quarter inches long, out of his leg. I don't think either of us gave this much thought in advance, if I did I imagined it meant locating the screws with some sort of geiger counter, making a little nick and taking a screw-driver to them. To Simon's surprise and disgust, he came round from the anaesthetic to find his leg was again in plaster to the knee. He was determined not to stop work, because he planned to leave for Smith Island in late July and there was a great deal to be done. After one day at home he told me to wake him as usual and left at a quarter past six. By about four o'clock he was home, pea green and with blood staining the plaster. Muttering that he must get to the bottom of this and find out what was under the plaster he sat on the kitchen floor with his little chipping hammer — something like a miniature ice axe — and started chipping the plaster away. Instead of five little nicks he found that the whole length of both original incisions had been reopened, one about twelve inches long running down the shin, another of about eight inches on the inner side of the leg from the ankle up. It seemed more politic for me to speak to Kenneth as Simon threatened to give him a piece of his mind, and we drove back to the hospital for the leg to be replastered. After that he took two days off, and I think spent one of them going to London to see various official people with whom he'd been in touch ever since he bought *En Avant*; from the correspondence I see that he first approached the Foreign Office Polar Regions Section in June '76, also Lord Shackleton, the Minister involved. Reading the letters one sees how amusement at the rather odd dishevelled young man stumping about in plaster and talking of fitting out an old wreck of a tug single-handed to take a non-existent crew to the Antarctic turned to respect and even affection, how 'Dear Mr Richardson' became 'My Dear Simon'. The first Foreign Office interdepartmental note that I have seen is headed 'Ephemera', which is what it must then have seemed. In March of '78, when things were a bit fraught and the search was at its height I had a very kind and concerned letter from Lord Shackleton wishing there was more he could do to help.

Early in December — we're back in '76 now — Major Tilman came to stay again after a disastrous voyage in *Baroque* when he had been forced to abandon her in Reykjavik. He was planning to find a crew to bring her home in May to sell her, fearing that 'increasing feebleness would oblige him to swallow the anchor some day, and that day was not far off.' Simon thought his wish was to die at sea, and was quite prepared if that happened to wrap him in an old sail and throw him overboard; he would be happy for the Old Man to sail with him until that did happen. At any rate, Major Tilman went down to Southampton to look at the rusty old tug, but he wisely didn't commit himself, preferring no doubt to wait and see how well Simon's plans materialized. Soon after this John was posted from Chatham, where his quarters had been exceedingly useful as a staging post between Stockbridge and Terneuzen, to Southampton and H.M.S. *Active* which was being built by Vosper Thorneycroft at their yard in the docks. The family — James was nine months old — moved into the Mill and John spent some of his leave helping Simon cutting and grinding in *En Avant*.

On Christmas Eve there was a disaster which could have wrecked all Simon's plans. We had friends coming for Christmas, and Simon decided to take three days off, but at seven in the morning Smithy telephoned to say that *En Avant* had sunk. As the boatyard was on tidal water, the boats lay over on their sides as the tide went out, to come up again as it made up. On this morning *En Avant* must have caught her coaming under that of her neighbour and instead of rising with the tide filled with filthy oily water and sank. Simon left at once and was not home until well after dark, dirty, wet and quite down. I had never seen him so down. All his tools and materials were damaged, some beyond repair. The part of the Lister generator which I'm told is called the commutator, and the coil of the Bosch steel-cutter had to be rewound, and some of the welding equipment had to be abandoned. By next morning he had quite recovered his equilibrium and played host as if he hadn't a care in the world; but by Boxing Day he had developed a horrible cough and cold. I suggested that it might be sensible to take a day off, but he said that if he didn't get down to it at once he might never face going back at all, and for the next few days worked through what looked and sounded like bronchitis, fortified by swigs of Benylin.

Soon after this, as if in compensation, something exciting happened: the expedition received Royal recognition. Early in February His Royal Highness the Duke of Edinburgh referred in a speech to the young men and women of Britain. He expressed concern that the spirit of adventure was not as strong as he would have liked and he encouraged young people everywhere not to be content with the second-rate but to live adventurously. I saw this reported in *The Times* and suggested that Simon wrote telling the Duke of the plans for the expedition, to reassure him that there were still young people of spirit in Britain. Simon agreed, just to humour me, and a carefully worded letter was typed on the smart new writing-paper, which Will Carter had designed and printed at the Rampant Lions Press, and sent to Buckingham Palace. By return of post came an envelope with the royal crest, and when Simon came home and opened it Selina and I could see that it contained some sort of bombshell. Simon's reaction to all good news was an incredulous 'I don't believe it', which he repeated several times before handing over the letter for us to share. It was from Lord Rupert Nevill:

BUCKINGHAM PALACE
20th February 1977

Dear Mr Richardson,

The Duke of Edinburgh has asked me to thank you for your letter of 7th February about the 1977 Smith Island Expedition.

His Royal Highness will be considering his recommendations for the Royal Society of St George Expedition Awards early in April when I shall be pleased to again lay your letter before him. I hope to be able to let you know soon afterwards whether or not Prince Philip has found it possible to support your expedition.

I would be grateful if you could let me have further details of the expedition.

Yours sincerely
Rupert Nevill

S. G. Richardson, Esq.

Simon sat down that evening and wrote a description of *En Avant* and a summary of his plans and sent it off at once.

BUCKINGHAM PALACE
19th April 1977

Dear Mr Richardson,

Further to my previous letters, I am delighted to have to tell you that the Duke of Edinburgh has been pleased to recommend the 1977 Smith Island Expedition for a 1977 Royal Society of St George Expedition Award.

A cheque for £150 will be sent to you by the Royal Society within the next few days.

Yours sincerely,
Rupert Nevill

S. G. Richardson, Esq.

From then on I typed 'Supported by the Royal Society of St George' on the writing paper. I must confess that I began to be anxious about who Simon was going to find to go with him on this expedition, though I kept it to myself. Simon had put an enormous amount of effort into it, now he had drawn public attention to it, and still there was no crew. He planned to leave — had to leave if he was to reach Smith Island and leave again before the Antarctic winter — in late July. I hated the thought that he might have to give up, though at heart I knew that if Simon wanted to do something it usually got done. I knew that Mark was the first choice of second in command, that Simon had invited him and had told him that until the last minute the place would be kept for him. Mark was by now a second mate, navigator, in the Merchant Navy, and much as he liked the idea he felt he could not face a whole year in such a small vessel. Major Tilman would not be back from Reykjavik until mid June, and his plans depended on selling *Baroque*. Simon was in touch with an Australian doctor, Trevor Davies, who was sailing his own boat back to England and had said he would join, but all that was heard from him was an occasional air-letter; and when one came from Capetown saying he had got engaged to be married when he arrived in England it seemed unlikely that he would immediately want to sail off for a year. Simon had asked Ilan Rosengarten, whose company and cooking he had enjoyed in *Baroque*, but Ilan was settled and working in Australia, as was Colin Putt — Tilman's friend Putto.

Simon needed climbers. Since being told that he himself would never climb again I suppose he felt that the next best thing would be to get someone else to the top of a mountain, and Mount Foster on Smith Island was an attractive unknown quantity — what Major Tilman had once described as 'a rich prize for someone'. Very little is known about Mount Foster. I still have some aerial photographs taken by Hunting Survey from which Major Tilman and Simon agreed that it might be an impossible climb or just possibly it might be a long gentle ice walk to the top. Simon, in a television interview before he left, described it as 'a mountain that requires climbing'; I think for him it was the symbol of an ideal.

At the end of April Simon put an advertisement in the General Vacancies of *The Times*:

Crew wanted for Antarctic Voyage 0264 81 525

To his dismay, for he had planned that it should appear on a Monday morning, it came out the previous Saturday, not the best day, he thought, for job-hunting. Before leaving in the morning, he asked casually if either Selina or I would be in, in case there were any replies. He went off to work telling us to ask anyone who was interested to write giving details of themselves, and said, as an afterthought, 'No psychologists and no sociologists'. At about half past seven the first call came. I took the name and address and brief classification and gave our address. By nine o'clock Selina and I were taking turns at the telephone; as soon as the receiver was put down the bell rang again. Several women rang, either diffident or aggressive about their femininity, and we said as long as they weren't either psychologists or sociologists we had no reason to believe they wouldn't be considered. In fact, a surprising number of both groups did ring, and we had to tell them of the ban. One imagined a crew made up entirely of people studying each other's behaviour, a thought which must have occurred to Simon. By the time he came home the pile of names and addresses had grown. We said nothing until curiosity, or perhaps anxiety, got the better of him, and he asked if anyone had answered his advertisement. Advertisement? we said, oh yes, and gave him the lists, which produced the characteristic 'I don't believe it'. I can't be sure how many there were on the first day, but altogether there were 168 replies spread over three or four days. The telephone never stopped ringing as many people tried to speak to Simon in the evening. About fifteen of the applicants were women, and Simon was dubious about taking any for two reasons: the possibility that Major Tilman might join him, and would certainly not want to sail with a woman in such primitive conditions, and, as Simon said, 'If a man breaks a leg you can say "Too bad, chum" and offer him some morphia, but if a woman does I should have to turn back.' A few applicants were merchant seamen thinking it was a paid job, and some weren't interested when they heard more about it. Many weren't remotely suitable, but there were quite enough promising applicants to reassure me that Simon wouldn't be sailing off alone. One enterprising girl called Eleanor Bloom, who worked at *The Times* newsdesk, followed up the advertisement, came down for a night to meet Simon, and wrote an article which *The Times* published on June 22nd.

Simon spent every evening writing and telephoning to the rest, and several came down to stay: from these he chose three, and offered them places. They were Rod Coatman, Robert Toombs, and Charles Williams. *En Avant* by this time was very different from the shabby old wreck that Jo Stevens knew. Simon had finished the keel, put up a 44-foot steel mast just aft of the bulkhead dividing the cabin from the engine room, fitted six good bunks in the cabin — the top two hinged to provide seating below — and generally made the whole thing habitable. The water tank had a teak top with a deep rim, or fiddles, to stop things sliding off. An old Esse solid fuel cooker, which he had been given by a friend wanting to go over to oil, had been installed in the cabin and a chimney made for it. Simon found a firm in Brighton who made conversion units, and they let him have one for the special price of, I think, £25.00. Our builder offered a choice of old stainless steel sinks which clients had thrown out, and Simon plumbed one in by the cabin door — the doorway which he had enlarged since we were in Holland and kept hitting our heads on. The engine room had been decked over, a lavatory installed, and Simon had contrived what he called the Captain's Cabin in a tiny space behind the engine room. This consisted of a chart table with drawers underneath, the rexine seat from the Saab that I had slept on in Terneuzen, a small cupboard and an old upholstered chair that had been in the nursery. Very snug, except that, unlike the cabin, it had no form of heating and only the steel hull between the occupant and the elements.

The sails had been ordered. These were Simon's one extravagance, his pride and joy, a suit of the finest flax sails from Jim Rawlings of 'G' Sails in Southampton. He chose the firm, 'G' Sails, I think, because Jim Rawlings still held, like Simon, that flax was in every way superior to modern materials, and had been chosen to make the sails for the modern *Mayflower*. A dislike of all plastics and substitutes was part of Simon's philosophy and he had none in his ship. He told a television interviewer that he thought he had been born a hundred years too late and would have been content to sail under the conditions available then; in fact, as far as possible, he tried to. Jim Rawlings was a big man in every sense of the word, and proved a good friend to Simon. He agreed to have the sails ready by the third week of July at a cost of £1,200. He has since died suddenly at the age of forty-seven, but his wife Freda remembers Simon and Mark — who must have been on leave — arriving at the loft. They were so covered in grease and dirt that she put down a mat just inside the door and asked them not to step off it into the sail loft. At first neither of them took the two young men seriously, the idea of converting a tug to sail and setting off for the Antarctic was ludicrous, but Jim Rawlings realized that they knew what they were talking about and were serious. The adventure appealed to him, and he welcomed an order for flax although it caused extra work as the material is only 24 inches wide. When Simon collected the sails, ready on time, he was only asked £1,000 on the grounds that making them had provided training for an apprentice; but I suspect it was Jim Rawlings' form of sponsorship. Freda Rawlings, when I later went to meet her, good-naturedly looked out the specifications for the sails (see Appendix I), which may be of interest to designers of sailing ships.

I had been given the job of making six new mattresses to fit the bunks, two foot wide and shaped to fit. I bought miles of striped ticking, black and white, and managed to beg or buy enough old horsehair mattresses to use for stuffing. Teasing out the horsehair was a filthy occupation because of the dust and dirt that came with it, and I tied up my hair and wore a mask, but it wasn't difficult. I buttoned them at intervals with an enormous trussing needle, and Simon was quite pleased with the result. Each person also had a long ticking roll, the length of the mattress and about ten inches across, which was all the space for gear they were to be allowed, and a ticking lee-board to stop them rolling out of the bunk.

From January to June John and Simon travelled to Southampton together every morning, Simon looking like a ruffian and John sitting on a pile of newspapers to protect his suit. Sometimes at lunchtime Simon joined the officers of H.M.S. *Active*, not yet in commission, and Selina and I, with John's parents, John and Ann Musters, went to sing 'Eternal Father, Strong To Save' in our smartest clothes and had lunch on the Quarter Deck. Then we walked across to where Simon's boat (see Appendix II), minute in comparison, lay moored below. In my heart I had included it in the hymns and prayers.

Robert Toombs was the first of the crew to join, in fact the only one who came to stay while John was still here. Robert was twenty-one, the son of Peter Toombs, a retired Major in the Royal Corps of Signals, and his wife Diane. They live and farm near Sherborne and have an older married daughter. Robert was at Sherborne School and went on to do a degree course in architecture at Oxford Polytechnic. At this time he was doing a year's practical work in a tanning factory before another two years in Oxford prior to the R.I.B.A. exams. He was a member of the sailing club at Sherborne, had a glider pilot's licence, and had done some climbing and potholing. One of his interests was a study of the Southern Albatross, so for a variety of reasons he wanted to join Simon. He gave his employers a month's notice, coming down to work at weekends until the time was up.

Rod Coatman was twenty-two, the younger son of John Coatman, an architect, and his wife Maureen, a sculptor. They lived near Aylesbury and Rod went from the Dragon School in Oxford to Pembroke College, where he read metallurgy and became a shooting blue. He was a good cook of the wholefood variety and had some sailing experience. Simon offered him the place of cook and Rod gave notice to the firm for whom he was working and came down towards the end of June.

Charles Williams was thirty-one, son of Mary Williams, a widow with another son and a daughter, both married, who lives in Singleton in Sussex. Charles went to Bedford School, leaving after O-levels because he was impatient to get out into the world and travel and explore. First he went with a friend and a canoe to Peru, crossed the Andes and came down the Amazon camping with the canoe. Then he worked in Iceland, leading parties for a firm called Minitrek, then spent several years with a similar job in the Sahara. Charles had climbed and sailed. He started coming down during the week and went home at weekends, arriving back on Sunday evenings with delicious little offerings of cakes and quiches which made us praise his mother's cooking. Charles was very keen on independence and self-sufficiency; he bought a trio of rabbits to breed fresh meat — 'You'll have to kill them,' said Rod, who was horrified at the idea — and built two very grand hutches for them, so each doe could have her own apartment, I suppose, and share the company of the buck, though later he found that rabbits didn't live like that and the does were put in together, with the wretched buck on the weather side of the boat that took all the water. Charles also took a variety of fishing tackle. One evening Simon came back from Southampton very amused because Charles had confessed that he was in fact married and it was his wife Sonnie who sent him back on Sunday with the splendid tuck. He had kept it a secret in case Simon was against taking married men. After that Sonnie came down at weekends and helped with the stores which became the responsibility of the women of the growing household. I also invited Julia Whately, the young artist friend, to move in and help with the work, and her talents both as cook and artist were tremendously helpful.

There was a great deal to do. The four men, with Mark's occasional help, were busy turning *En Avant* into a comfortable ship. Simon was offered a quantity of insulating material, in large sheets, by a firm in Gravesend, which I collected in two loads with a hired Ford Transit van; and soon the whole cabin, sides and ceiling, was insulated. It was very hot that July, and working inside was uncomfortable, but Rod told me that as they went on with the work of insulating the cabin it became noticeably cooler in there. Shelves were put up in every available space, such wiring as was necessary was done and then the cabin was panelled and painted. They were very pleased with their work.

We were equally busy at home. Selina had James to look after, but catering is her subject; she has a Higher National Diploma in Catering and Hotel Management, and we were certainly a hotel. I woke the four men at a quarter to six every morning and cooked an enormous breakfast, and, while they ate, the women cut sandwiches for their lunch. Before Simon left he gave me my instructions for the day: letters to be written to suppliers and things to be collected. Selina was asked to work out how much food eight men would need for a year, and I was given the delicate task of approaching manufacturers with the hope of sponsorship. At about six in the evening the van, which was beginning to look very battered, rattled down the drive and the kitchen filled with dirty, hungry men who consumed several loaves of bread with butter and jam and drank pot after pot of tea. At eight or half past we put the main meal on the table, quantity rather than quality, and the evening was spent sitting round the table discussing the day and making plans for the next. By common consent we lived in the kitchen in an attempt to confine the dirt and oil, and I still have a particular affection for the vinyl tablecloth with its brown and white pattern engrained all round the edge with darker brown. It reminds me of many happy evenings, because I became very fond of them all.

During this time *En Avant* was moved from Smithy's yard to the docks for the last stages of the work. I had stopped considering the fact that there were still only four men instead of eight, it seemed as if nothing could stop Simon's plans now. On 19 June Major Tilman wrote to say that he had brought *Baroque* back to England, had sold her to a man who was going to restore her as a Bristol Pilot Cutter of her period, that he would join Simon and *En Avant* and come down as soon as he had made arrangements for Toff, his dog. We were all delighted at the news, perhaps for different reasons: I because it meant that this experienced old man, who knew Simon, had seen *En Avant* at her worst, and above all who knew the conditions which she might meet on her voyage south, felt this was a reasonable undertaking. Simon impressed on us all at that the last thing Major Tilman would want was any sort of publicity, and when he made two television appearances in the next few weeks he made no mention of his distinguished companion. At the end of the month Major Tilman arrived, and from then on put in a full day's work with the others, scraping, scrubbing and painting. At dead low tide the way on and off *En Avant* was by way of a rope dangling below the short iron ladder down from the quay. I remember Rod describing to me one evening the incredible ease with which the seventy-nine-year-old climber managed this, gathering himself together at the bottom and then mounting smoothly hand over hand up the rope.

Rod was endearingly generous with his praise at all times, telling me once that it was incredible to him that Simon was only twenty-four because he had such mature authority. He marvelled too at Major Tilman's stamina on the day shortly before they sailed when *En Avant* was slipped out of the water for a coat of anti-fouling paint: he stood in his wellies in the mud from seven-thirty in the morning until evening painting the hull above his head. A problem arose as to what the distinguished old man should be called. Simon had solved this before he arrived by writing to say that as his usual term of 'Skipper' no longer applied, he'd be glad to know what it was to be in the future. He was invited to use the wartime name of 'Tilly', but, as Rod said, that didn't apply to the crew, who avoided calling him anything at all. I suggested that if they all called him Major Tilman they would soon find out what he wanted; it worked, and the next evening they came home delighted that they had all been invited to call him Tilly. They all respected and admired him tremendously, even affectionately, though he would be embarrassed to hear me say so, and in subsequent letters home this was apparent: 'Tilly is a really tremendous person. He continues in his own way, and the more I get to know him the more obvious it becomes how he has achieved so much in his life.' 'Tilly really is a remarkable man. I saw him take a really heavy fall this morning and, apart from a few oaths, he didn't turn a hair. Most men of seventy-nine would, I think, have taken some days to recover. He seems to be completely at ease on a boat and moves around with a sort of nonchalant air while we are still clinging to the nearest object.'

Major Tilman — I was never invited to call him Tilly, nor would I have wanted to — 's arrival was a great encouragement though Simon behaved as if it was what he expected. He seemed completely unruffled by the fact that he still needed three more men and was within four or five weeks of leaving. He needed at least two good climbers, and when the expected letter came from Trevor Davies saying that he must after all pull out as his new wife didn't want him to be away for so long it was a compensation that he offered the name of an American climber who might be interested. This was twenty-eight-year-old Joe Dittamore who was on his way from Alaska to England and would get in touch when he arrived. We had no idea how or when he would arrive, nor was Simon prepared to take him if he didn't seem suitable. A couple of days later a young American voice on the telephone announced itself as belonging to Joe Dittamore who was at Andover station. I felt from the moment I heard him that Joe was going to be the right person, and the fact that he had got himself to Andover without expecting to be met at Heathrow or Gatwick was very encouraging. I went off at once to collect him and Simon arrived home in the evening to find that he now had a crew of six. Joe was from Effingham, Illinois, a ski and climbing instructor who had been working in Alaska, and although he hadn't much sailing experience Simon had no doubts about his suitability. He had great charm and simplicity and would have got on well with anyone. Most climbers wouldn't want to spend an uncomfortable year sailing to and from an unknown mountain, but I think Joe welcomed the adventure and the active life. An added bonus was that he had a New Zealand friend, a climber, who might be interested in joining them in the Falklands. Simon wrote immediately to this man.

Soon after Joe arrived Simon had his last, and in many ways, best, piece of news. We were at supper one evening when the telephone rang. Rod went to answer it and called Simon: it was Mark, ringing from Cornwall. Simon came back and, without any show of jubilation, said 'Mark's coming with us. I knew he would.' Although subsequently I have felt very keenly for Michael and Jean having lost two sons, I think that the relationship between Mark and Simon was as good as is humanly possible; I don't ever remember them arguing or falling out, and they seemed to communicate without words. They led charmed lives of great value and deserved not to grow old or tired. Mark's decision was welcomed by all the crew, including Major Tilman. He came the next day, and though he didn't of course live with us he often ate here and Jean and Michael were very hospitable to the crew.

From then on work gathered momentum, the final touches were put everywhere, the sails delivered and the rigging finished. Word of their imminent departure went round the docks and Authority in the form of the Board of Trade appeared. This annoyed Simon because a considerable charge was made for an examination of *En Avant*, but to our relief — I didn't at the time realize what a good thing this was — she was passed as sound provided that a second hatch was made forward; even Simon had to agree that this was reasonable, and he made it virtually overnight. The next day he and Mark, with Major Tilman and his friend Sandy Lee, who had been helping, took the boat into the Solent to swing the compass. They found that the steel mast was giving considerable interference in its position beside the compass, and Sandy did a beautiful piece of carpentry and made it a sort of beehive well forward, with a canvas cover that looked just like a wedding cake.

I set off for Surrey to collect some radio equipment, lent by Decca, and an eight man inflatable life-raft which was my contribution to the expedition. Another thing which Simon felt he needed was a rifle. He gave me the address of an armaments dealer — in Manchester, I think it was — and told me to write asking if they had any second-hand. To his surprise they wrote back asking what he would like, to choose something he would like as a present. I thought before we started importing lethal weapons into the Mill I had better find out about licencing regulations, so I went down to talk to our friendly neighbourhood policeman. Simon had a shotgun certificate, and was a good shot, as were Mark and Charles, and Rod of course was a blue, but rifles were another matter. Sergeant Hatcher was quite positive: as Simon was the Master of a sea-going vessel he was entitled automatic-ally to a licence to keep a rifle on board, but until he sailed there were certain precautions he should take if it was kept in the house. This apparently also applied to the possession of drugs like morphia, and Michael prescribed various things which he thought they should take. I wrote to Manchester asking for a Lee Enfield 303 and a few days later it arrived by Securicor, with several hundred rounds of ammunition. As far as I know only one shot was fired from it, as we heard from

Charles, Mark and Simon. Charles wrote a graphic description of how he and Mark were swimming on a 'damnably' hot day in a millpond sea, Mark in goggles. Suddenly Mark shouted 'shark' which precipitated them back to the boat, where everyone was rushing for the rifle, rods, harpoons and knives. Charles found a gash-bucket and threw it overboard just as the ominous dorsal fin was breaking the surface, then he baited his rod with a lump of squid the size of a fist and waited. For half an hour nothing happened, and they started lunch; then they heard the sound of the reel running out. Charles played the shark alongside — which he must have enjoyed — then Simon harpooned it, and Rod killed it with one skilful shot into the spine just below the head. It was a blue shark, about four foot long and weighing about 70 lbs. Mark said they ate it and it tasted like putrid leather, Simon simply said it was very flabby.

Apart from the rifle, I wrote lots of letters to other manufacturers, and we had a much better response than even Simon hoped for. The women were kept busy at home; Selina cooked cake after cake, solid twelve inch fruit cakes, which she sealed into three large plastic drums which Robert got from the tannery where he had worked. Julia painted all the tins as they arrived to stop them from rusting in the bilges, where Simon planned to store them, then marked them with the contents. Simon brought home a gallon of orange paint and half a gallon of grey which, as he described it, had fallen off a crane. Apparently little offerings were deposited for him on the quayside by sympathetic dock workers. A crane or a truck would drive up, *En Avant* would be hailed, and he would come on deck to find a vehicle driving away leaving a little present of nails, paint, or whatever behind. The bottom of the Mill soon became a storehouse, and my mini had to live outside, as Selina and Julia arranged everything in orderly rows.

It was amazing how much was given. William sent a beast from the farm in Somerset to our local abattoir and I had to collect it one very hot day. Simon wanted to use all the traditional ways of preserving food, as he couldn't have a freezer, and I was told to set about salting beef. With the help of Dorothy Hartley's *Food in England* I collected recipes and diagrams of smoke houses, salting equipment and pickling tubs. Luckily all this turned out to be unnecessary, because when I mentioned it to the manager of the abattoir he not only volunteered to have all the suitable joints pickled by an old man there who had worked as a butcher all his life and knew how to preserve meat, but said that he had a friend in a meat canning factory who would tin all the stewing beef for us. This was a great relief, and Julia soon had rows of tins painted orange with STEW in dark grey.

Provisioning eight men for a year was not an easy task. Each man had contributed a sum — I think it was £400 but am not sure — for food and fuel on the expedition, and Selina worked out the quantities they would need. Then Simon added on a bit for luck, because he thought food was vital to success. I wrote letters to everyone we could think of, on the expedition paper, 'For or on behalf of Simon Richardson, leader of the expedition', and I thought it better not to ask for free gifts, but for advice. This worked wonderfully. Some of the paper had a synopsis of the plans on the back, and I would write something like, 'You will appreciate the difficulties of storing perishables in the extremes of temperatures through which the expedition will pass. Can you advise me how long your product will last under these conditions?' Or 'How much lavatory paper will be required by eight men for a year?' It was obviously the right approach. A firm of bacon curers had twelve specially cured hams cured and packed for us, and asked in return only that they should be able to photograph them being loaded on board for the firm's newssheet. Another bacon curer in Norfolk, with whom I had many pleasant conversations, not only sent four cases of double-vacuum-packed best back bacon labelled grandly SMITH ISLAND EXPEDITION 1977, but also arranged with the wholesaler from whom we collected it that we should be allowed to buy any other provisions we needed at wholesale rates, an enormous saving. When the manufacturers of loo paper wrote that they would give the appropriate amount Simon, instead of being deeply grateful, told me to write back at once to say that he didn't want 'greaseproof', our name for the old shiny stuff; but luckily, before I had worked out how to do this without damaging the rugged explorer image, a van drove up and unloaded crates and crates of something labelled 'Babysoft' in pastel shades of pink, blue and yellow. Biscuits arrived by the vanload, and an enormous quantity of spices which Rod had begged from somewhere, including five pounds of cayenne pepper; this must have been a joke, and they took about an ounce and left the rest for me to dispose of.

I made one friend, with whom I've since exchanged Christmas cards but never met, the owner of a watermill like ours, that still produces wholemeal flour. This dear man, after several telephone conversations — I worked out early on that the best time to chat people up was between half past four and five in the afternoon, the time when they could decently leave their offices — offered to give and pack in special sacks a sufficient supply for the expedition, including one sack of white 'for birthdays and Christmas'. I told him all about Selina's fruit cakes, and that she was packing icing sugar and candles, and we got on to the subject of young people and how good they were and quite up to the standards we were brought up with. When I saw his firm's paper, I found that he had an M.C., and I hope that the thought that there were still young people willing and able to face hardship and danger pleased him. Another firm producing blackcurrant syrup gave 24 litres — 'the crew are particularly anxious to avoid scurvy. Can you tell me if the intense heat in the tropics will affect the Vitamin C content?' — and the director of a firm importing Hungarian red peppers delivered a boot-load on his way to Lymington to sail. It proved very difficult to find either tinned butter or full-cream dried milk in England, 'even for ready money' and both had to be specially imported and were very expensive.

Simon wanted the rice and other dried things like pasta and beans packed in linen bags so that they could be stored in odd corners; Selina cut up some old nursery curtains and a kind neighbour helped to machine drawstring bags. We worked out a good system of storage: for each of the various goods we had a two-litre ice-cream box — we had eaten our way through a vast quantity of ice-cream — with the name painted on it, and strokes to indicate the number of bags still in store. Each time the box was refilled Rod was to cross off one stroke, so in theory he would always know how much was left.

About a week before they were due to leave, while Julia was hanging upside down over the stern of *En Avant* painting her name and port of registration, Rod set off in a three-ton hired van for a wholefood co-operative in north London and bought boxes of beautiful dried fruits, peaches and pears and apricots, as well as kidney beans and brown rice and lentils. Selina and I meanwhile drove to the wholesaler in Aldershot, where Rod met us, and we bought all the rest of the stores. We had a very long list and took our time over it. At lunchtime we went to the delicatessen department and bought pies and drinks, and sat on our trolleys having a picnic. The four cases of Norfolk bacon with their SMITH ISLAND 1977 labels attracted a lot of attention, and we had a brief moment of reflected glory. That night we put a padlock on the Mill. The next day Selina and James left for Plymouth to join John, so they missed the most exciting day of all, the day Simon sailed.

The day before Simon told me to be ready to help him pack his clothes in the afternoon. In the morning I was to go to Southampton to buy him one of those unattractive peaked Francis Chichester caps. At the last minute he had accepted the fact that, like all my family, his eyes couldn't stand bright light, and the glare at sea can be purgatory. He despised dark glasses and wouldn't wear them, and he probably had a struggle with himself before he sent me off to buy the cap. I laid it on his bed in the attic with all his other clothes and we filled his dittybag. It held so little, and I imagined what they would look like at the end of a year. The rejected clothes I put away in his drawers, and suddenly the room looked strangely tidy and empty, and I think I realized then that he was going away for a long time and that we might not be alone together before he went. I said, 'I don't expect any news of you, don't think you have to write to send messages. I'll expect you back in a year.' 'A year and a day, actually,' he said 'because of income tax.' We both knew there wouldn't be any goodbyes, and I said, 'Stand still for a minute' and put my arms round him and my head on his shoulder. There was absolutely no response at all, neither an answering pressure nor a withdrawal, which was as it should be. It reminded me of an occasion when he had said, 'I really resent being tied to this house and you', and I had replied indignantly, 'You aren't tied to me.' 'I am, damn you,' he said.

The morning of 8 August started early. Simon's Saab van, which by now was on its very last legs, had to make two journeys to Southampton to carry the crew and their gear; *En Avant* was to sail on the tide at eight o'clock so first breakfast was at four-thirty — bacon, eggs, sausages, tomatoes and mushrooms. Second breakfast at five-thirty. Maureen Coatman was with us, and Paddy had arrived the evening before to see them off, and he and I were to go on the way to the vegetable market to stock the ship with fresh vegetables. William was cutting his corn, but had come earlier, between haymaking and harvest, to see progress.

It was a gorgeous morning. The vegetable market opened at half past six and Paddy and I filled his Rover with potatoes, cabbages, cauliflowers, lettuces, tomatoes, everything we could lay hands on. When we arrived at the quayside it must have been about half past seven. Michael, Jean, Clare and Hal were already there. *En Avant* was looking her very best and a small crowd had gathered round her. A reporter whom we christened The Gorilla because he was about six foot four and bearded was talking to Simon, there was at least one press photographer, and I remember that a foreman from Vosper was plaintively calling for any Vosper electricians to start work. One of the Board of Trade men was pointed out to me, and several from the Docks Board. A small boat brought more sightseers. Simon left the reporter and came up to me and said 'I'm off now'. He was wearing a brown knitted cap that Jean had made for him — his going away hat he called it — and one of Dicky's dark blue Viyella sailing shirts. I noticed a silver chain round his neck which I had never seen him wear before, and found when I got home that the chain with Dicky's naval identity discs was missing. He said 'I'm off now' and I said 'Have a lovely time' and he was gone. All the others were already aboard except Rod who was on the quay talking to Maureen. Simon called him, saying, 'If you're coming you'd better come. We're Off.' Joe ran up the rigging and hugged me, I knelt on the quay and kissed Robert. Hal Johnson was making a cine film: he started in the bow calling each of them in turn and they looked round and smiled at the camera. When he reached Simon and called his name, Simon didn't turn but leant forward and started the Deutz. Water rushed out from under *En Avant*'s stern and she pulled slowly away from the quay. It was exactly eight o'clock. We watched her turn into the fairway past some moored yachts and out into the main channel and I hoped she would find enough wind to hoist her sails. Our plan was to drive with our picnic lunch down to Hurst Castle where the main channel comes in close to the beach and see them sail past. The Solent never looked lovelier. There was a slight heat haze and in the distance we could see the Needles. We settled down to wait, and it must have been about half past eleven when Clare with binoculars picked up *En Avant* making steadily towards us, and as she came nearer they could see us — one of the slides which came back from Rio shows us all sitting on the shore — and stood on deck waving, Joe as usual up the rigging. My only regret was that there was not a breath of wind so I never saw *En Avant* with her sails set.

Our picnic lunch was very happy. Someone had lugged a bottle of plonk along the mile and a half of shingle to Hurst Castle and we drank to *En Avant*'s voyage and to the health of the crew and then to ourselves and felt very united. When at last we broke up Paddy dropped me back at the docks on his way home. The quay was looking very empty with *En Avant* gone, and I drove the Saab home in fear and trembling that I might be caught with four bald tyres, no brakes, several insecure parts and committing heaven knows what other motoring offences.

Longstock Mill felt utterly deserted after the excitement of the last eight months. I was now going to live there quite alone except for my mongrel collie. It must have been about six o'clock and I thought I would have a bath and a very early bed. Luckily I had had the bath, and some supper as well, before the telephone rang summoning me to Winchester Hospital. I had quite forgotten Lynn. She was a young girl living in the Quaker Meeting House who had fallen in with an older man, a drug addict and burglar, who was now back in prison leaving her pregnant. Her parents didn't live in England and I had promised that, as she had no one, I would be with her for the birth. I drove into Winchester and was with her until her daughter was born at about eleven-thirty, an extraordinary calm and beautiful birth with a relaxed and happy mother. It was a wonderful end to a creative day. Lynn and her baby joined her family in Canada, and every Christmas I get a card that reminds me of all the emotions I felt in those twenty-odd hours.

29/30 August

Dear Mrs R,

There is very little to say really. The postmark on the letter and date shows that we had an excellent run down to here. Nothing untoward has happened. E.A. has not rolled over, sunk, blown up or anything else, in fact she has behaved excellently, perhaps a slight disinterest in being so far from home. Bar Rod and Joe we are all very fit. They are still suffering from sea sickness, which worries me, and them too. Robert has been doing most of the cooking. . . .

We motored most of the way out of the Channel and it was not until south of Lisbon that we picked up the good weather that will now continue till south of Rio. We expect to be in Rio by the beginning of November, perhaps the end of October and then the Falklands by the end of November/beginning of December. I am particularly avoiding all communication with the outside world so that you will not hear till a letter from Rio.

There is only one thing that I can think of that we have forgotten and that is sail needles. Sail needles are just the same as leather three-cornered ones. The size I want are I think size 16. If you telephone Mrs Rawlings, the fat sailmaker's wife in Southampton, 4 Pitt Road (see Yellow Pages under 'Sailmakers' — 'G' Sailmakers Ltd — she will have them. I want them for stitching canvas and terylene about the same thickness as the mattress covers, perhaps a little thicker. Say a dozen assorted sizes. Also on the shopping list from that surplus store in Southampton, 2 Primus stoves — the ones we have not being too bright. From Borden or wherever, another 20 Tilley mantles and 3 Tilley 'service packs' S.P.1's, like the ones you bought before. Also I believe that 'Primus' Ltd make kits for the primus stoves in the way of spare burners and pumps. The new complete stoves that you get should cover our needs but if you come across the spares a comprehensive collection would not come amiss.

The food is excellent, but the salt beef and hams are a little indigestible. We have yet to open a tin of corn and Tilly and I have opened the first tin of peppers today. I think that we will have 1 ton left when we get back.

I cannot think of much to say except that all is well, especially since the customs have not even bothered to come aboard to look at the rabbits — the black and white doe having lost all but one of her litter. The buck was looking very sorry for himself after half a gale off Finistère, when he was flooded out a few times, but soon recovered when let loose.

I have not yet had a change or wash of clothes and have not yet gone ashore. I did however shave yesterday p.m. We shall have sailed by the time you get this so for now goodbye and bon chance with the premium bonds. Also on the shopping list is a lump of beeswax, a fistful. It wants to be very hard stuff. Mrs Rawlings again will have this or Bertie. Could you tell Mrs Rawlings also how delighted we are with the sails — a treat to look at and use. Can think of little else to say so adieu.

Simon

I tried repeatedly to telephone but have been unable to get through. Joe has a New Zealander who is almost definitely going to meet us in the Falklands. This means that I can take one other at Rio — either Allan or his friend. At Rio we should know whether Allan or the N.Z. are definite and whether it's possible to take Allan and his friend. The earliest date that we will be in Rio is Oct. 15 — however I suspect that the end of the month more likely.

On 29 October the telephone rang and the familiar voice said 'Good morning'. I said 'Good afternoon', realizing that Simon must be in Rio. He gave me a list of things he wanted me to do and told me that two New Zealand climbers were joining him in Port Stanley, Joe's friend and another. He hoped to be there in early December, about the 6th. I asked about the water supplies, because I knew he had thought they might have to be rationed on the long leg from Las Palmas, and he said his arrangements for catching rain in sails had worked very well and there'd been no problem. He was very pleased with the way *En Avant* had behaved and he 'couldn't wait to get into the really rough stuff'. I told him that the two cases of supplies — through the kindness of Lord Shackleton the Falkland Island Company had agreed to ship them out free for him — had been loaded and would be waiting. The last thing he told me, which at the time I didn't particularly take notice of, was that he had decided to go down the coast rather than straight on across to the Falklands. He didn't say why, but he repeated it, so later I realized it had some special significance. He said it had been a very good trip and I said I'd see him on 10 August next year.

Letter from Simon Richardson to Angus Clarke from Rio

Yacht Club, Rio
October 1977

I have sat in some member's seat and worn my home-made Southern Ocean hat in this club and the Commodore has disapproved and we are now not allowed to walk on marble. Unbelievably this is the most expensive club in the world — no yachts. If your skin is not white (or light brown) you are not allowed in. A South African boat came in with a black crew member and the whole crew was — dare I say it? — blacked . . . an extraordinary place altogether but like all S.A., worth seeing. To be able to afford to buy coffee is of course an added luxury at 30/– a kilo. Seeing Sugar Loaf from the sea, after 65 days in the desolate ocean has its charm, coupled with this it was the day that I finished converting the Esse to oilfired, to my mild surprise it worked and baked its first loaf, that means that we will be warm down south. I have seen the trade winds and doldrums, in a beam trade wind *En Avant* will carry full sail in 30 knots of wind with no problem, in the doldrums saltwater poured slowly on the deck boils easily. My first albatross. We caught a blue shark in a sea full of squid blowing water and ink, if caught, all over one. Otherwise the tropic ocean is devoid of life and only the sweet and cool of the night can make it tolerable. The trade winds are the pleasure of ocean sailing. How *En Avant* will like the Southern Ocean, only time will tell. So far she hasn't betrayed any faults, taken rough weather with a shake and a bound, as if loving it. So my dream is over. It would have been worth the terrible struggle just to get this far. I have started planning my next dream. She's 110 feet long, built to be frozen into ice and can carry 100 tons of cargo and only the wheel and mast extending above deck level. I will build this one and go on a circumnavigation via the N.W. Passage and Pacific.

Mark, who has neither mutinied nor gone mad, and I are planning to lock up charts and sextants on the trip home to see if we can get to the Channel with no aids from Tristan da Cunha. We leave in a day or two. If you hear from an Argentinian port all will not be well — otherwise six weeks to Port Stanley, where the natives should be friendly.

All regards to family,
Simon.

Letter from Rio to Christopher Lloyd Owen

25th October

Chris,

What excellent news I hear from Angus and *The Times*. You have beaten us all by a long chalk. I must however be honest and admit that my first thought was that I must now surely be able to get free spare parts for my engine. The thought did not last long and I soon realised that although missing the great day, I would probably not be invited owing to my uncouth travelling habits. My love to you and please find enclosed cheque enough to buy a bottle of whisky towards your great voyage to come. I never thanked you for one you sent me. How we left on that far far away day I don't know, but we did and with your help.

I expect you are not particularly interested in doldrums, trade winds, sailing tugs — the post mark shows that we got here. What else is there to say except such horrible details? I have seen much, travelled far, but few stories of tempests, only stories of hot calms under tropic skies — the deck so hot that it boiled seawater. My first albatross, skua, booby — swallows even, sharks, dolphin, whales and sunsets. I seem at this stage to be held in great respect, which I hope will continue, not for my ashamed ego but for the happiness of all. I have already designed and built and sailed my next boat and will soon start on the third and last by the way home.

The next leg to the Falklands will be the one of greatest interest. We will then find out whether we will make it to the south. *En Avant* sails like a dream with greatest mileage in a day of 132, a good sea boat but perhaps not good enough for the great southern ocean. The day we arrived here was perhaps the greatest day of my life. I had just completed converting the Esse to ship's use and it worked and we saw land after 65 days in our cell existence. If everything ended now, life would have been worth that day.

All speed and love

Simon.

Letter from Rio

Rio Yacht Club
29.10.77

Dear Mrs R.

Rio, this place is fantastic, but hopeless for anything — rather like Italy with a touch of next week, month, year — manana does not enter into it. You have to sit and wait for days to telephone. You cannot post anything in and out of the country however. We arrived quietly slowly and safely — too long in the doldrums, wherever they are. Two climbers from N.Z. are en route for P. Stanley and will be there in 2 weeks — so they should be waiting for us. I would forget this chap especially if he can only get to Palmer Base since there is no earthly possibility of us getting there until the end of April, if we manage to get there at all. Should be in Falklands by beginning of December if all goes well. I have written to Palmer Base commander. If a letter gets from here to there it will be a miracle, but one can try. The telephone today was about £20+ which is not surprising but worth it. We have managed to get our free beer and will leave on Monday. 5 weeks at best to Stanley. The last half will be the most interesting of the whole trip to see if *En Avant* likes rough weather. I have not seen any nasty habits but the proof is in the pudding.

About the chronometer. The one we bought is absolutely useless, except that we have found out how it is incorrect, but there is no reason why K. Hughes should not get us a new one to P.S. I wrote to their office in Soton, just inside Gate 4. If you can trace the letter, preferably to the M.D. and make sure that they pull their finger out. Instruct them however that I will accept a new free one but will under *no circumstances* buy a new one and wait to get my money back when I return the old one. What is more you can explain politely that what they call a chronometer has no relation to what a chronometer is, i.e. a machine that tells accurately time at all times, does not stop, and one where it is possible to tell what minute of the hour. I explained all this politely in the letter, but they will need a bomb under them. However let no money pass hands since I can buy one in the Falklands of a decent make, i.e. not English. I must not get my bloodpressure up, however it would be an interesting court case if *En Avant* was lost owing to an inherent fault of design of a chronometer. Even the dictionary describes it as a time keeping machine specially for the use of determining longitude at sea, interesting.

Many thanks for all those X-words, they will keep the navigators happy for many an hour. Nothing has gone wrong. We had a third of our water left after a fast run from the equator. Will write from P. Stanley

love   Simon.

JUST AS SIMON was heading towards the 'really rough stuff' so at this point of the narrative am I. By the spring of 1983 I had got this far when a completely unexpected caller rang my doorbell and introduced himself as Geoffrey Hattersley-Smith, a name I recognized from the days when we were beginning to realize that *En Avant* was overdue at the Falklands and something might have gone wrong. He stood on the doorstep and said 'I promised myself that if ever I was in Hampshire I would come and tell you how much I admired your son.' I was completely disarmed and welcomed him in. I'd always hoped to meet some of the people who had been so helpful and sensitive through that very difficult period: the three names I particularly remembered were John Heap of the Polar Region Section of the Foreign Office, his assistant Christine Bloomfield, and Geoffrey Hattersley-Smith of the British Antarctic Survey working in the Foreign Office. Simon had caused them a lot of extra work and worry yet they seemed genuinely concerned for the safety of the expedition, which had saved me a lot of anxiety. To think that one of them had remembered him nearly seven years later was very touching. I told Geoffrey Hattersley-Smith that I was sorry that I hadn't met John Heap to thank him and the upshot was that I was invited to lunch with them both in June. When I told them that I was writing this book John Heap provided me with all the unclassified information on file.

Simon had expected to be in Port Stanley early in December. His plan was to pick up the New Zealand climbers and the stores and go straight on down to Smith Island in the South Shetlands, the chain between Cape Horn and the Antarctic Peninsula. The climbers would be put ashore to make their way with their supplies up the sheer ice cliffs of the island, while the others took *En Avant* to Deception Island to do any necessary repairs before collecting the climbers again and sailing for home via Tristan da Cunha and St Helena. They carried the Decca transmitter with a range of a thousand miles, a Racal Squadcall which broadcast a distress signal, and short range equipment so that the climbing party could keep in touch.

Towards Christmas I became aware of tension building up among the families of the crew — telephone calls asking if I'd had any news, speculation about the delay and tentative enquiries whether I thought anything should be done. Not wanting to seem anxious I took it all

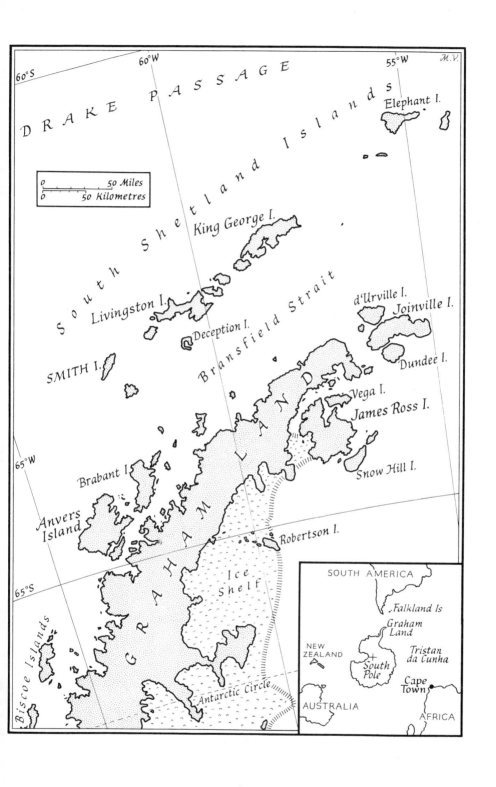

lightly, which, looking back, may have been infuriating to some, but seemed best at the time. An exciting parcel arrived from Kodak, four boxes of colour slides taken on the way down to Rio, showing *En Avant* in all weather and everyone looking very happy: dolphins playing, stormy seas breaking over the bow, Joe mending sails, Robert reading by lamplight, Rod putting bread to rise in the sun and Simon in a Robinson Crusoe hat made of sailcloth — the Southern Ocean hat of Angus' letter — at the helm against a cloudless sky. There are two sequences I particularly like: one of Major Tilman and Mark taking sunsights, dressed in shorts which slip lower and lower as they stand holding their arms up, the other of a birthday party in the cabin, Rod holding first what looks like a plate of ring doughnuts, then an iced birthday cake covered in candles, then Simon blowing out the candles. September 24th, his twenty-fifth birthday.

Christmas came and went and no news. One afternoon in early January my telephone rang. I sat at my desk in the dining room in the dusk and heard the operator telling me to hold on for a call from the Falkland Islands. I held on for several long minutes, my heart thumping, thinking that soon I would be speaking to Simon and then I could telephone to call the other families telling them that all was well. Then with a lot of crackling a strange voice announced itself as one of the New Zealanders, asking me what I thought they should do, should they hang on there or should they give up? It was a frightful let-down, and I didn't think quickly enough to say that by now there could be no hope of getting to Smith Island in time to attempt the climb before they had to leave; I said I thought it was too soon to give up.

Shortly after this I had two telephone calls which were the beginning of the most unpleasant part of the whole venture. The first was from someone called Jack Hill of the *Daily Express* from Southampton, who wanted an interview with me and was belligerently abrasive when I said I had no news to give him. The second was from Tim Hurst of B.B.C. South, who had met Simon when he was interviewed before leaving, and was friendly and interested. I didn't know what had started this publicity, so I telephoned and spoke to Christine Bloomfield at the Foreign Office. Within an hour John Heap rang back, having found the explanation. The New Zealander in the Falklands had immediately got in touch with Robert Lawrie, the retired climber with a shop near Marble Arch, and told him that *En Avant* was overdue and that H. W. Tilman and the expedition were lost. This piece of 'news' was announced at a dinner of the Alpine Club somewhere in the North. John Heap advised me to tell any other reporters who rang that I was in touch with the Foreign Office who were aware of the situation, that I thought the rumours alarmist, and that I would let them know if there were any news. It was interesting throughout that all the climbers were convinced after a week or so that all hope should be abandoned, whereas the sailors knew of many instances of explorers being out of touch for months — Shackleton for years — and turning up safely in the end.

On 9 January the search for *En Avant* began. All British Antarctic Survey ships were asked by the Captain of H.M.S. *Endurance* to keep a lookout, and the Argentinian and Chilean air services were informed. I remembered Simon on the telephone from Rio telling me that he had decided to go down the coast of South America, which I told John Heap, and the significance of it suddenly struck me. If he were behind schedule, and I believed he was, partly through the original delay in sailing and partly because of being becalmed in the doldrums, then he might have thought that the call in to the Falklands would have to be cut out. There were two climbers there; but it would be pointless to go out of his way to pick them up if by doing so he was too late to attempt the climb. By going down the coast I felt he might be keeping the option open of taking the shortest possible route to Smith Island. There were the two crates of food to be picked up; but he had said there was masses of food on board, and I knew he had been told — I suppose by B.A.S. — that a recent expedition to Elephant Island had abandoned stocks of food and supplies there which he was welcome to help himself to, and he could pick these up for the voyage home. The more I looked at the map and the more I thought of Simon telling me of this change of plan, which must have been for a reason, the more likely it seemed. When I heard, I can't remember at what stage, that Simon had told the Harbour authorities when he sailed from Rio on 1 November that he was 'bound for Antarctica' it seemed to confirm this theory. Admittedly this was a more romantic way of putting it, very much in keeping with Simon's image, but it was not strictly speaking true if he were bound for the Falklands. I tried to keep an open mind. The climbers would feel let down but I didn't think Simon would abandon the expedition to pick them up for nothing, it would not be reasonable. John Heap was a source of strength throughout, he never made me feel that I was being a nuisance; at one point he gave me his home telephone number in case of emergency, which was noble of him. Towards the end of February he had to go to the Argentine, and he wrote to let me know that he would be away for a month. He ended his letter: 'The outlook for Simon is beginning to look a bit bleak but we should remember that he has ample food and supplies aboard *En Avant*, and like you I think it is reasonable to hope that Simon will turn up somewhere asking what all the fuss has been about.'

By 3 March I was being plagued by reporters, and so I rang Christine Bloomfield again and she spoke with the press department of the Foreign Office and I was told to issue the following statement, which I did:

> Some disquiet is being felt for the members of the British Smith Island Expedition which left Southampton on 9 August to make the first climbing ascent of a point on the mountainous Smith Island in the South Shetland group. The small expedition of seven has as one of its members the experienced mountaineer and ocean voyager Major Tilman; the leader is Simon Richardson of Stockbridge in Hampshire, who has sailed with Major Tilman previously in Arctic waters. They left Southampton in a 65ft sloop which he had converted to sail from its original purpose of a tug designed to sail in ice. The expedition, which has the backing of the Royal Society of St George, reached Rio de Janeiro on 1 November. Since leaving Rio no news has been received and it is assumed that conditions have forced them to change their plans.

I was to go on saying that I wasn't worried by the lack of news.

I think the *Daily Express* had already published something about *En Avant*, because I got several aggressive calls from reporters, and I think all the tabloid papers tried to get interviews. It became so unpleasant that I stopped saying who I was to callers. I had to answer the telephone because I was alone in the house and I might have missed something from Simon, or news of him, so I always asked the caller's name and said 'I'm afraid that Mrs Richardson is not available', and put the receiver down. Sometimes this was the end of it, but I learnt a few of the tricks of the trade. After I had rung off a few minutes would elapse, then the bell would ring again and a different voice would start straight off with 'Mrs Richardson I wonder if you could — ' and I would say 'Mrs Richardson is not available' and put the receiver down. Again a bit later a voice would ask 'Dorothy?' and when I asked who it was it would be a reporter — or a female voice would exclaim

'Dorothy!' in a How-lovely-to-find-you-in voice. It became quite difficult to keep up the po-faced stock reply. Once my bedside telephone rang at three in the morning and a voice asked what I had to say to the news that my son was dead. My first thought was that a body had been washed up somewhere, but I realized that I would have had some official news first, and I managed to say 'I have no reason to believe that my son is dead'.

Two or three days later a friend showed me an article out of the *Daily Mail* of 20 March written over the name Malcolm Stuart. Under a banner headline 'I Know My Son is Alive, says Mother' there was an article headed 'Mother Refuses to Give Up after Five Months Silence' purporting to be an interview with me at home 'a converted Mill house in Hampshire', putting into my mouth such unlikely words as 'I am convinced that within a month or two they will be in touch to say the whole mission has been a success' and 'These days we are too expectant of instant communication'. I began to feel rather vexed with Simon for exposing me to this, though I knew it was unreasonable of me, and it was just anger at the people who were harassing me. A little later on, when I was beginning to wish very much for news, another reporter telephoned. I said my usual bit about not being available, and then — I can't remember exactly the words he used but he definitely gave me to understand that he had news of Simon that he would give me when I admitted who I was. I remember the lift of excitement before I realized that it was another trick. Looking back, I still find it hard to believe that anyone is prepared to act like this, even to feel it's clever, to earn a living so brutally.

The thought that a body might have been washed up made me realize that I was the only person who knew them all well enough to identify one of them if this should happen, and I faced the fact that I might find myself being taken to some South American mortuary to look at a body that might have been in the water for some time to see if it was one of the seven men who had left my house in such high spirits. When I took the dogs out into the garden last thing at night I used to look up at the stars and feel that the answer to the question that was always in my mind lay somewhere there — was Simon somewhere looking up into the same sky?

One evening it occurred to me that I hadn't considered the possibility of telepathy, which Dicky and I had brought to a fine art in moments of emergency. If Simon was in difficulty somewhere perhaps he was thinking of me. Having lived for a month in *En Avant* I

knew exactly what it felt like in the cabin, and I knew all the crew. I sat
alone by the fire and I remembered the cabin and I thought of each
member of the crew in turn, what they looked like and how they
spoke, and I imagined them sitting round the table. Nothing came
back to me, absolutely nothing at all. I don't really think I expected
that it would. It was late, so I put the fire to bed, laid my breakfast tray
and started upstairs to bed. It was my habit to switch off the
downstairs lights and walk upstairs in the dark, because we have made
some alterations in the house since the wiring was done and the
switches are in the wrong places. Having lived here so long I feel quite
at home in the dark, and I often don't bother with lights. I switched
them all off, and started up the stairs. I had got nearly to the top of the
first flight, just before the little half-landing leading off to my
bathroom and bedroom, when I was seized by an extraordinary
feeling: it was as if I had walked into a different world, and I had a
conviction of absolute peace and rightness. It was so tangible that the
memory of it is still in that place. It was as if I had walked into it and
was held in calm and peace. I went on upstairs, through the bathroom
in the dark and into my bedroom where the curtains were not drawn. I
still didn't put on the lights, as if that would break the spell, and I
walked across my room to the window and looked out. There was a
full moon. Instead of the garden and the river and the water meadows
outside, there was calm unbroken sea — no trees, no church spire, no
river, nothing but calm peaceful sea and the moon shining. I didn't
know what it meant but I knew all was well, all manner of things were
well, and I didn't need to try to explain it to myself. I was just grateful
for it. That step on the stairs became associated with the conviction of
goodness and has remained so. Once or twice when things became
really difficult I went and sat on the step and remembered and felt
supported. Even now I know that world still exists.

This experience kept me going through the next few months, which
were pretty tough. I was determined to keep an open mind and not to
be seen to give up too soon, mainly, I confess, because I could imagine
Simon's reaction if I did. Whoever said 'Anxiety doesn't rob
tomorrow of its sorrow, it only robs today of its strength' had a strong
point; I chose to think only of the best possibilities and not dwell on
horrors. If they had gone straight to Smith Island they would have to
leave by the end of March, and might arrive in South Georgia by the
end of April. I discovered that there was no permanent base on South

Georgia, some Argentinians in the north but no permanent British base, so Simon would not necessarily put in there. His next port of call would be St Helena which would take several more weeks.

There were no facts at all. Our concern was based entirely on the absence of news. No wreckage, no bodies, no distress calls. I remembered how pleased they all were with the Decca Voyager when I brought it home, and I think Simon said it had a range of a thousand miles. The Racal Squadcall was designed for emergencies; if thrown into the water it would broadcast its position for 24 hours on an international waveband. Of course, someone would have to be there to pick up the signal, and I had no idea of the distance involved. I imagine the Antarctic as one enormous uncharted expanse of ice and small islands, cold and calm and silent. I know that it is possible to survive for longer there than in the Arctic because there are seals and penguins, but that's about all I know. I just felt for the sake of the other parents that I had to appear unworried and I was determined Simon shouldn't catch me out.

On April 14th a signal was sent from H.M.S. *Endurance* to say that between 23 February and 15 March a helicopter search had been carried out on Smith Island and no trace of men or a landing had been seen. Another disappointment but still negative, and I reasoned that one fall of snow would obliterate all tracks. Major Tilman's friends in Australia, Colin Putt and David Lewis, both experienced sailors, drew up a report of their assessment of the situation. Headed 'Comments on the Disappearance of *En Avant*', it concluded that it was highly probable in the first instance that she had been disabled rather than sunk and might be drifting towards the coast of Africa. They sent this report to the Royal Institute of Navigation and the Director, Michael Richey, got in touch with me and invited me to a meeting of experts to decide what should be done. I felt that the last thing they would want was an unknown mother there — most inhibiting — so I asked our solicitor-sailor friend, Merton Naydler, who had introduced Simon to Major Tilman in the first place, to go instead. I collected all the information which I thought might be useful, including a blown-up photograph of the rudder and steering which they seemed to think the most likely source of disablement.

On 24 April the Royal Institute of Navigation put out an international warning to all shipping and air services. I had had a very kind letter from Lord Shackleton when the publicity started offering to help in any way possible; he was in Australia at this time and arrangements were made through Michael Richey for him to meet David Lewis and Colin Putt. On 4 July a second meeting took place in London between Michael Richey, John Heap and Merton Naydler, and a decision was made to put the following into operation immediately:

1. A further Navigational Warning, alerting shipping and aviation, to be sent out through the office of the Hydrographer to the Royal Navy.
2. Michael Richey would, through Lord Shackleton or the British Ambassador in Washington, ascertain the possibility of tracing *En Avant*'s progress from the time she left Rio, by satellite pictures.
3. John Heap, who was shortly going to the Argentine, would sound out the Argentinians on the possibility of an air search in the South Shetland Islands area as soon as flying resumed, probably not until early November.

This report quoted the latest Australian notes:

. . . it must be emphasized that hope for the crew's survival has not disappeared and there is still a strong case for attempts to find and rescue them. On many occasions in the last 70 years groups of men who have lost their ship or other logistic support in the Antarctic have demonstrated that it is entirely possible then to survive for a year or more living chiefly off the country. Men with the outstanding resourcefulness of Tilman and Richardson should find no difficulty in doing likewise. Further action towards an eventual rescue is therefore strongly recommended.

All that summer and into the autumn I was in a curious state of limbo. If it hadn't been for the conviction that all was well, whether Simon was dead or alive all was well, it would have been very difficult. Most of the other families had given up hope, I think, finding the strain of uncertainty intolerable, but I doggedly stuck to the possibilities confirmed by those men who knew the sea and the conditions in the Antarctic. Simon would have liked nothing better than to have come home and been able to laugh at me for giving him up too soon. I was not going to allow him the opportunity. Sometimes I indulged in a harmless little vice of imagining a telephone call beginning with the familiar 'Good Morning'. 'There'll be six extra to dinner', and I would say, 'Well, it'll only be spaghetti bolognese. If you want fillet steak you should have warned me.' I knew it was unreal, but it wasn't hurting anyone, so there was no harm in it.

In November the Foreign Office sent copies of the memorandum to the Embassies and High Commissions of Argentina, Australia, Chile, France, Japan, New Zealand, Norway, Poland, South Africa, U.S.A. and the U.S.S.R., thanking them for the great efforts that had already been made and asking them to continue to keep a watch for survivors or any evidence of the fate of *En Avant*. At the end of the year a decision had to be made about the crates which were still waiting in the Falklands. As I had a Power of Attorney for Simon I was able to write asking that the contents should be sold at auction and the proceeds put to any charity nominated by the Governor. In due course I had a most sensitive and appreciative letter from H.E. Mr J. R. W. Parker, thanking me and telling me that the sum of £660 had been given to the King Edward Memorial Hospital in Port Stanley as a memorial to the Expedition. I like to think it helped the wounded in the Falklands war.

On 22 January, 1979, John Heap was at the fiftieth Anniversary Dinner of the Antarctic Club, and wrote to me the next day: 'There is one solemn moment at each dinner when a Silent Toast is drunk "To those who have voyaged to the Antarctic Regions and have not returned." I, and I am sure a number of others, thought most especially of Simon and his friends.'

I am very grateful to John Heap for that letter. Not only because it put Simon and his crew into a very select little band, but that it gave me a positive cut-off point in thinking he might still come home. Although Major Tilman's family didn't get a legal presumption of death until April 1979, and his obituary wasn't published by *The Times* until the following November, John Heap's letter gave me a logical reason for accepting the fact of Simon's death. A friend who never knew him, one of the many men who seem to find a great interest in the story of Simon's life, asked me if I have never felt grief for his loss. I could honestly say I haven't. I do know what grief is like and I have experienced it several times; but not for Simon. I have never dreamt that he came back, I have never heard his voice nor thought I saw him in the street, nor have I felt depression and despair. For Simon it would be irrelevant and self-indulgent, because he was free and I gladly let him go. The day he sailed I almost burst with pride, and that pride is with me still. It's a humbling thought that if I had not miscarried our first boy Simon might never have been born.

The two questions I was asked by John Mead in the television interview and my answers I quote from the transcript:

'What do you think yourself probably happened?'

'I think that they met something, that they were overwhelmed. In fact I feel reasonably sure, as much as anybody can say, I think that they were overwhelmed by these rough seas that Simon couldn't wait to get into, which simply overwhelmed them, so that they could neither put out a distress call, nor could they throw into the water their Racal Squadcall which would have gone on automatically putting out a distress signal. It must have been something catastrophic that simply overwhelmed the whole boat.'

'How do you remember, how would you like other people to remember, perhaps is a better way of putting it, Simon and all of them and that last voyage?'

'Well, they were a splendid collection of young, enthusiastic men who wanted very much to go. There was one old man of enormous experience, who wanted to go on being adventurous to the end of his life, and I think he was as glad to go with them as they were to have him. They went off on a beautiful day, they had a marvellous sail to Rio, because in the letter from Rio Simon actually says "If we get no further than this, it will all have been worth it." And it seems to me that is a splendid way of living your life, whether you're, as he was, twenty-five, or as Major Tilman was, seventy-nine, what on earth more does any of us want? So I think that what we know they all achieved was a tremendous achievement, and I'm very glad to remember them all as they went then.'

That, I suppose, is the end of Simon's story, but it isn't quite the end of mine. I have spent a lot of the last three years talking to people who knew Simon well, and I don't think I have learned anything new about him, but everything I felt instinctively has been confirmed. One detail that has struck me forcibly is the number, men and women, young and old, who have actually said 'I loved Simon'. Is this unusual? I don't know. I have always loved him, but I could understand anyone who found him tiresome; he refused to accept any limitation, so the precise might find him slapdash, the pedantic undisciplined, the conventional loutish, and I wouldn't blame them. To find so many actually saying, with no trace of awkwardness, 'I loved him' has been very rewarding. Looking back, I would say that the relationship between us was entirely satisfying, it was complete, and this, I think, is why I was able to face the months of anxiety when he was missing and his eventual loss without being annihilated, and why I don't mourn him. Whatever was right for Simon would happen and I have no complaint.

Two of my sayings from way back come to me: 'if ever I were in a tight corner Simon is the person I'd most like to have with me', and 'only a fool would worry about Simon'. I had just about finished writing this book when someone turned up from the past who helped me to crystallize my thought — Janine Barbereau, who came to us as an *au pair* when Simon was ten months old and stayed for nine months. She never heard him speak. I know she was happy here and loved him dearly, and, though she had not seen him for twenty odd years, the news of his death was a great sadness to her. Janine talked to me of her memories of Simon, and something she said gave me an insight into what I was looking for. 'He enjoyed meeting other children,' she said. 'He was very sociable, and when inevitably another child took the toy he was playing with he never got angry, he was perfectly happy to take another toy; but he would give the thief a rather scornful smile. He was essentially a well-balanced child, always contented. In France we would say he was "bien dans sa peau".' We in England haven't a good idiom for 'bien dans sa peau', the nearest I can get is 'at ease with himself' which isn't quite good enough, but it exactly fits Simon at every stage of his life. Janine recognized this quality in the infant she knew, and nothing in his life damaged it. The essential free spirit that we all are at birth grew and reached its potential early because that freedom was never limited or conditioned. Simon's determination not to be held back by involvement with any other human was not entirely easy to accept, but I hope I understood it when I made the gesture of release just before he sailed: he needed to let the wind blow between himself and those he loved, and he went as a free human being; unpossessive and unpossessed.

I had finished this book, as I thought, when I came across the piece of Rainer Maria Rilke which I have quoted at its opening, and it seemed to crystallize all that I have been thinking and writing. This essential distance between people is something which Simon understood very well, as did Dicky, and which I have come to understand in my own quest. That he loved many people I do not doubt — he was a very affectionate and loving child — and he lived wonderfully, side by side with us: but he allowed us the dignity of being ourselves, whole people, not appendages of himself. I have written of him with diffidence, not as 'my son' but rather as 'his mother'. Between these two attitudes there is a world of difference, the immeasurable distance that has enabled me to see, and perhaps to show, Simon 'whole against the sky'.

LONGSTOCK MILL   DOROTHY RICHARDSON
1985

APPENDIX I

SAILS

A set 1275	Mr Richardson En Avant			8 June 1977

	Mainsail	784 sq. ft		77642
24″ flax R.N.4	Luff	24′0″	23′7″	
	Foot	29′8″	$-2\frac{3}{4}$ round 29′ 5$\frac{1}{2}$	
	Leach	43′6″	42′8″	
	Head	22′2″	22′2″	
	Throat			
	diagonal	37′2″	$-36′5\frac{1}{2}$	
	Head			
	diagonal	43′ 10$\frac{1}{2}$		
Vertical cut	2 rows reefs (6′0 LUFF $-6′6″$ at leach)			
Laced foot				5–6 July, 1977
	Staysail	243 sq. ft		77643
24″ flax R.N.3	Luff	33′0		
	Leach	27′3		
	Foot	18′0		
Vertical cut	1 reef (6′0)			11 July
	Jib			77644
24″ flax R.N.4		226 sq. ft		
	Luff	37′8		
	Leach	24′10		
	Foot	18′3 $-$		

APPENDIX II

En Avant: gaff rigged sloop

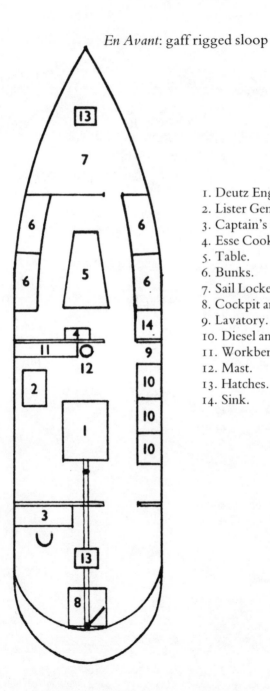

1. Deutz Engine.
2. Lister Generator.
3. Captain's Cabin.
4. Esse Cooker.
5. Table.
6. Bunks.
7. Sail Locker.
8. Cockpit and Tiller.
9. Lavatory.
10. Diesel and Paraffin Tanks.
11. Workbench.
12. Mast.
13. Hatches.
14. Sink.

APPENDIX III

COMMENTS ON THE DISAPPEARANCE OF *EN AVANT*

by Colin Putt and David Lewis

THE CONVERTED TUG *En Avant* has failed to arrive at an agreed time and place, and there is now a tendency, especially among those who have no experience of the Southern Ocean or of small, old ships, to write her off, with her crew. Fortunately, the situation is not so simple.

En Avant is a small tug hull, built of steel, converted to cutter rig and re-engined with an old, simple, low-powered compression-ignition engine. Tug hulls are both deep and beamy as power vessels go, with considerable stability, even to the point of carrying sail effectively, although this ability may be limited by the usually low freeboard which limits the amount of ballast which can be carried. A strongly constructed hull of this type, like *En Avant*, should be very resistant to the worst effects of a knockdown or broach-to in a big sea, and at 62 feet overall length she is rather big to be pitchpoled end over end by a large sea. Thus, although the sea conditions in Drake's Passage, where she was bound, can be and often are very bad, *En Avant* was by no means unfitted for them.

On the other hand power hulls, and even tug hulls, are notoriously unhandy when converted to sail: they lack the stiffness, freeboard, and lateral resistance which are required especially when sailing to windward, and at the best they tend to be slow and unweatherly. If partly disabled by loss of masts, spars, or sails, or even if forced to shorten sail drastically, they can lose not only the ability to make good to windward, but also quite possibly the ability to be steered and sailed at all. Conrad gave a telling description of this effect in a small steam ship equipped with sails, in his story 'Falk'. A small ship, undertaking a long voyage and carrying a large crew and expedition stores and equipment, cannot carry enough fuel to use engines as a substitute for sail if sail fails her.

The conclusion from the above is, that it is highly probable that the disappearance of *En Avant* is due in the first instance to her having been disabled rather than sunk. There must therefore be a strong possibility that her crew are still alive, and action should be taken to rescue them if possible.

The possibilities and probabilities of the various mishaps which could have come to the ship since leaving Rio, late in 1977, seem to be as follows:

She was bound for Port Stanley, did not arrive in December as planned to pick up two more men, and has not been heard of since. There are three main possibilities after leaving Rio: the ship has foundered, or she has been disabled, or finding progress slow and the ship unable to hold against the great winds and seas of the higher latitudes South, her crew have decided to hold any distance they still had to windward, abandon the call at Port Stanley, and head directly across Drake's passage for their objective, the South Shetland islands. The relative probabilities of these three possibilities are judged to be about 30:40:30.

If there was a next leg to the voyage, with the ship fully under command, it would then have been from somewhere between Rio and Port Stanley, toward Smith Island in the South Shetlands. Again on this leg there was the possibility that the ship might be overwhelmed and founder, or again, she might have been disabled. Or she could have been wrecked on an island, the Antarctic mainland, or in ice. The probabilities of these three events are judged to be, relatively, 33:34:33. Compounding these probabilities together according to the laws of chance, the overall probabilities become:

Foundered	30 + 10 = 40	
Disabled	40 + 10 = 50	
Wrecked	10 = 10	
TOTAL	100%	

The probability that the ship was disabled is very high, because at each stage there was a chance of disablement. If she has become disabled in the general area between the southern part of the American continent and the Antarctic Peninsula, the prevailing strong West winds and their accompanying currents would have made it impossible to get back to America, the Antarctic Peninsula, or the islands between, and seamen of Tilman's and Richardson's experience would not even try.

The idea of trying to land on one of the islands to leeward, such as South Georgia or the Falklands, appears more attractive at first sight, but to attempt a landing on the windward coasts would be most perilous, and even if En Avant were able to steer to one of these, arrival on such a lee shore in bad weather and in a disabled ship would be a thing to avoid at almost any cost.

Anyway, they have not turned up at South Georgia or the Falklands, and it is more likely that they have made such jury arrangements as they could and headed for Capetown. The Cape would be downwind and down current, a large target to aim for, and surrounded by shipping lanes. It is a long way, but it is at least practicable if the ship is capable of anything more than drifting. Even if drifting, the drift route would be past the Cape. Depending on their speed, they could now be getting near Capetown. On getting near the Cape, there will be difficulties with the Aghulas current which will tend to push them away again to the east and north, but by this time they are getting close to shipping lanes, and must depend on shipping for their eventual rescue.

If En Avant has foundered, and this is not impossible, there is nothing now that can be done for the crew.

She would have had to run the gauntlet of other risks to get wrecked, and therefore the probability of wreck is not high. However, if she has been wrecked, it is possible that some at least of the crew may be surviving ashore or on ice, but in this case the coming winter is likely to be the end of them.

Action can and must be taken to increase the chances that the crew may be rescued, as follows:

1. Ship disabled and heading for Capetown.
By now, food and water must be getting very short on board. There should be at least a little fuel left, and Richardson would have built an efficient still using this fuel to produce fresh water. As expedition supplies were carried, there should be enough food for a very short ration. It is now essential that all ships and aircraft in the areas between Drake's Passage and the Cape, and particularly those near the Cape, should be alerted to watch for a small vessel, possibly under jury rig or dismasted, and not necessarily making distress signals. (Both Tilman and Richardson are strongly averse to this sort of thing, especially if it could involve salvage claims, but they might by now accept offers of food, water, fuel, and transmission of messages.)

2. Ship wrecked, and crew surviving.

Here searches are called for, if at all possible, even though the situation is much less likely than disablement. The possible search area includes not only the South Shetland islands and the northern end of the Antarctic Peninsula, but also all land to the lee of these; the South Orkneys, South Georgia, and the Falklands. A search is a daunting task, the area is huge and the length of deeply indented and inaccessible coastline is enormous. A search from the sea would take years, and an air search is the only practical possibility, although the local conditions make this very difficult, too. Every effort should be made to have searches carried out by those who have suitable aircraft in the region. Within this possibility of shipwreck there is the smaller possibility that survivors are not ashore but drifting, in a boat or on ice. It is very hard to think of any effective action which could be taken in this rather unlikely case, except again to warn all shipping and aircraft in relevant areas to keep a good lookout.

17.4.78   DAVID LEWIS
                                                    C. K. PUTT

APPENDIX IV

Summary of Information Relating to the Possible Loss of *En Avant*

The Royal Institute of Navigation

1. THE PROJECT. Simon Richardson's purpose was to sail *En Avant* to the Antarctic and climb Mt Foster, the highest summit on Smith Island, 63°S. 62°W.

Sailing from Southampton in the summer of 1977 the expedition intended to leave Port Stanley in the Falkland Islands in December 1977 for Deception Island, 700 miles to the south and then go on to Smith Island, a further 60 miles to the west, where a party would be landed with provisions for three months, a radio, a rifle and distress flares. *En Avant* would return to Deception Island but maintain radio contact with Smith Island. She would return to Smith Island for the shore party early in February 1978; they would explore parts of the Graham Land peninsular and leave again for England in March, returning via South Georgia, Tristan da Cunha, St Helena, Ascension Island and the Azores, to be home by July.

2. THE BOAT. Registered as a British yacht just before she sailed from Southampton, *En Avant* is a small steel-hulled tug, built in Groningen in 1942, bought by Richardson in 1976 and converted by him for sail. She is gaff-cutter rigged, without a bowsprit: length 18 metres, beam 3 metres, draught 2.5 metres aft and 1.75 forward, strengthened with 15 mm steel plating at the waterline. The height of her steel mast is 13 metres above the deck. She has been fitted with an old, simple, low-powered compression-ignition engine and is believed to carry enough fuel for 2000 miles under power. She is understood to have been fitted with a counterbalanced rudder with a servo tab on the trailing edge to provide a simple form of automatic assisted steering. Her topsides were painted black, her deck grey, and her name was clearly painted on the bows and stern.

3. THE CREW. The known names of members of the expedition who sailed from Southampton in *En Avant* are:

> Simon Richardson (skipper)
> H. W. Tilman
> Mark Johnson
> Charles Williams
> Roderick Coatman
> Joe Dittamore (U.S. citizen)
> Robert Toombs

Two New Zealander climbers were contacted when Richardson was at Las Palmas and it was arranged that they would join the expedition when *En Avant* reached the Falkland Islands.

Richardson, an engineer, is an experienced yachtsman and climber. Tilman has a life-long experience of climbing, not only in the Himalayas but also in Patagonia, Greenland and Spitsbergen, and of sailing both in the Arctic and sub-Antarctic. Johnson (ex-Merchant Navy) is an experienced navigator.

4. THE VOYAGE. After some delay in fitting out and completing registration formalities, *En Avant* sailed from Southampton early in August 1977, and from Las Palmas in the Canary Islands at the beginning of September. She reached Rio de Janeiro on about 25 October after a comfortable voyage, as Tilman says: 'knocking off 100 miles a day for a week', after they picked up the S.E. Trades. Several letters were written from Rio to relations and friends and Richardson expressed a firm intention to call at Port Stanley to pick up the two New Zealander climbers. She sailed from Rio, probably on 1 November 1977. Nothing has been heard of her since.

5. SUBSEQUENT ACTION. In January 1978 Captain Wallis, R.N., commanding the Ice Patrol Ship H.M.S. *Endurance*, was officially asked to report any information concerning the whereabouts of *En Avant*. On January 24 he reported:

(i) Whereabouts of *En Avant* not known.
(ii) Two New Zealand climbers have been waiting in Port Stanley to join yacht since Oct/Nov. Also stores await collection.
(iii) Final destination Smith Island. Consider out of character for Richardson to proceed direct without picking up climbers.
(iv) B.A.S. ships and others have been requested to look-out.

A further report dated 13 March reads:

(i) Ship and helo search of most of Smith Island including planned landing place at Cape Smith carried out 12 Mar.

(ii) No sign of *En Avant* personnel nor indications that anyone has landed.

(iii) Deception Island not visited but discussion with A.R.A. *San Martin* 4 Mar indicates island deserted and no sign of yacht.

In view of the possibility that *En Avant* might be disabled or adrift in the South Atlantic, a navigational warning for Area 7, No. 028, was issued on 24 April 1978, by the South African authorities at the instance of the Hydrographer of the Navy. The British Antarctic Survey was aware of the situation, and they were in fact aware of Richardson's plans before he sailed.

6. THE POSSIBILITIES. An assessment of the possible implications of the lack of any news of the expedition was made in March 1978 by Dr David Lewis, himself eminently experienced in Antarctic navigation under sail, in collaboration with Dr Graham Budd and Mr Colin Putt. Copies were forwarded to the Royal Institute of Navigation, of which David Lewis is a Fellow and Gold Medallist; to the Royal Geographical Society, the Mount Everest Foundation and the Royal Cruising Club. It was subsequently agreed that the Royal Institute of Navigation would assume a co-ordinating role in the matter.

At a meeting held at the Royal Institute of Navigation between Frank George, Merton Naydler (a friend of the Richardson family) and Michael Richey, it was agreed to suggest that Lord Shackleton, who was already aware of the situation, should visit Dr Lewis while he was in Australia. As a result of this visit the conclusions were that *En Avant*:

(i) might have foundered, possibly between Rio and Port Stanley,

(ii) might have been wrecked on some Antarctic shore,

(iii) might be disabled and adrift in the South Atlantic.

These possibilities were discussed, in the light of all the information available, at a meeting with Frank George, John Heap (of the Foreign Office), Merton Naydler and Michael Richey held at the Royal Institute of Navigation on 4 July 1978. Although it may now seem more likely that *En Avant* foundered and that her crew are lost, it was felt that other possibilities should not be dismissed. If she was wrecked in the Antarctic, such an experienced party might well survive the southern winter and searches should be resumed in October or November. If she is disabled it is still possible that the boat, or the survivors, may be sighted by other ships or aircraft. The possibility of establishing the facts from satellite observations should also be borne in mind.

AUGUST 1978

INDEX